The Grammar of 'God' in Judaism, Christianity and Islam

T0270637

Key Concepts in Interreligious Discourses

Edited by
Georges Tamer

Volume 15

The Grammar of 'God' in Judaism, Christianity and Islam

Edited by
Farid Suleiman and Mira Sievers

DE GRUYTER

KCID Editorial Advisory Board:
Prof. Dr. Asma Afsaruddin; Prof. Dr. Nader El-Bizri; Prof. Dr. Patrice Brodeur;
Prof. Dr. Elisabeth Gräb-Schmidt; Dr. Naghmeh Jahan; Prof. Dr. Assaad Elias Kattan;
Prof. Dr. Christian Lange; Prof. Dr. Manfred Pirner; Prof. Dr. Nathanael Riemer;
Prof. Dr. Kenneth Seeskin

ISBN 978-3-11-150136-9
e-ISBN (PDF) 978-3-11-150161-1
e-ISBN (EPUB) 978-3-11-150231-1
ISSN 2513-1117

Library of Congress Control Number: 2024937627

Bibliographic information published by the Deutsche Nationalbibliothek
The Deutsche Nationalbibliothek lists this publication in the Deutsche Nationalbibliografie;
detailed bibliographic data are available on the Internet at http://dnb.dnb.de.

© 2024 Walter de Gruyter GmbH, Berlin/Boston
Typesetting: Integra Software Services Pvt. Ltd.

www.degruyter.com

Contents

Contents

Mira Sievers
Introduction
Jewish-Christian-Islamic Encounters through Wittgenstein's Lens:
Bridging the Gap between Religious Language and Theology

In recent years, theology in European and North American universities has faced increasing challenges. On the one hand, the transformative processes of the last decades have brought about greater social and religious diversity.[1] The concept of a multi-religious society now accurately describes the current reality in many countries where – due to the exercise of positive religious freedom – a variety of religions coexist, with the monotheistic faiths just being a part of this diverse tapestry.[2] This leads to increasingly frequent questions whether the discipline of theology, too, must represent this plurality. On the other hand, the academic relevance of theology as such and its place within universities is being questioned. As more people – exercising negative religious freedom – choose not to affiliate with any particular religion, there are concerns about the justification for allocating public resources to theological institutions at universities.[3] Despite the challenges, there are also notable developments that have strengthened the position of these institutions, exemplified by the recent establishment of centres for Jewish and Islamic theology at German universities.[4]

To react to these challenges, there has been a growing emphasis on interreligious dialogue in recent years, fostering also academic encounters of theologians and the engagement of different theological institutions in various forms. In this

---

1 Liedhegener, Antonius, "Pluralisierung," in: Detlef Pollack et al. (eds.), *Handbuch Religionssoziologie*, 347–382, Wiesbaden: Springer VS, 2018; Stackhouse, John G., "Religious Diversity, Secularization, and Postmodernity," in: Chad Meister (ed.), *The Oxford Handbook of Religious Diversity*, 239–249, Oxford: Oxford University Press, 2010.
2 Bernhardt, Reinhold, *Inter-Religio. Das Christentum in Beziehung zu anderen Religionen*, Zürich: TVZ, 2019, 73–76; Stackhouse, "Religious Diversity," published online: https://doi.org/10.1093/oxfordhb/9780195340136.003.0018 (accessed on 10.01.2024).
3 Even though the theory of secularization has been heavily criticized, it is still frequently used to explain current developments. See Pollack, Detlef, "Säkularisierung," in: Detlef Pollack et al. (eds.), *Handbuch Religionssoziologie*, 303–327, Wiesbaden: Springer VS, 2018; Dobbelaere, Karel, "The Meaning and Scope of Secularization," in: Peter B. Clarke (ed.), *The Oxford Handbook of the Sociology of Religion*, Oxford: Oxford University Press, 2009.
4 Following the recommendations of the German Council of Science and Humanities in 2010, Wissenschaftsrat (ed.), *Empfehlungen zur Weiterentwicklung von Theologien und religionsbezogenen Wissenschaften an deutschen Hochschulen*, Berlin/Köln, 2010, https://www.wissenschaftsrat.de/download/archiv/9678-10.html (accessed on 10.01.2024).

https://doi.org/10.1515/9783111501611-001

context, chairs dedicated to the study of "Abrahamic religions" have been established, for example at the Universities of Oxford and Cambridge in the United Kingdom.[5] Additionally, experiments with interfaith religious education have been conducted in public schools, as can be seen in an institutionalised form in Hamburg in Germany.[6] Also in Germany, in Berlin, academic theologies of different religions are aligning themselves institutionally.[7] Alongside reflecting on social changes and jointly exploring theological and societal inquiries, these initiatives are certainly driven by the hope to gather collective strength, aiming to showcase and communicate the relevance of theology to a broader public.

But on what grounds can the three religious traditions of Judaism, Christianity, and Islam come together academically? A common starting point often revolves around theological questions that emerge from their shared engagement with Greek philosophy, which has influenced these three religions and their respective theologies in distinct ways. For instance, topics such as theodicy, concepts of revelation, and religious anthropology are discussed and set into relation with each other. Greek-influenced philosophy frequently serves as a common ground – as "figure of the third" – acting as a bridge that transcends the boundaries of the individual religious traditions, enabling fruitful exchanges.[8] However, it is not uncommon for critics to accuse such theological reflection of being disconnected from real-life concerns or overly abstract. As a matter of fact, certain questions concerning the interplay between the foundational religious texts, the actual beliefs and practices of the faithful, and the Greek-influenced theological reflections persist without immediate resolution: Unresolved questions, such as the coherent reconciliation of human free will and divine predestination, await

---

5 The concept of "Abrahamic religions" (and therefore also "Abrahamic Studies") is not uncontroversial. For the development of terminology and criticism see Silk, Mark, "The Abrahamic Religions as a Modern Concept," in: Adam J. Silverstein/Guy G. Stroumsa (eds.), *The Oxford Handbook of the Abrahamic Religions*, 71–87, Oxford: Oxford University Press, 2005.

6 Bauer, Jochen, *Religionsunterricht für alle. Eine multitheologische Fachdidaktik*, Stuttgart: Kohlhammer, 2019, 14–45.

7 In January 2023, the Jewish, Christian and Islamic theological institutions at the University of Potsdam and the Humboldt University Berlin began their collaboration in the interdisciplinary center *Religious Traditions in Transformations*.

8 For a study on the "Figure of the third" and its uses see Eßlinger, Eva et al. (eds.), *Die Figur des Dritten. Ein kulturwissenschaftliches Paradigma*, Frankfurt am Main: Suhrkamp, 2010, especially 25f. For a special reference of this concept to interreligious dialogue see Krochmalnik, Daniel, "Trialog 'in unserer Zeit' (Nostra Aetate). Ein Beitrag zum Weiterdenken der Konzilserklärung," in: Reinhold Boschki/Josef Wohlmuth (eds.), *Nostra Aetate 4*, 207–214, Leiden: Brill/Schöningh, 2015.

answers at an uncertain point in the future – a situation that makes some critics doubt the relevance of this kind of interreligious engagement.

To address this challenge and bridge the gap between religious convictions and philosophical contemplation, this edited volume adopts a distinct approach by taking the later philosophy of Wittgenstein as a new "figure of the third."[9] Ludwig Wittgenstein was born in Vienna in 1889. After studying at the Technische Hochschule in Berlin-Charlottenburg he continued his studies in the United Kingdom and soon moved to Cambridge to study with Bertrand Russell, focussing on philosophy and the foundations of logic. His first book, the *Tractatus Logico-Philosophicus* was published after his service in World War I in Austria. After a break from philosophy, he returned to England in 1929 where he worked on *Philosophical Investigations* which was published only posthumously. He died in Cambridge in 1951.

Wittgenstein's thinking is currently being received in a wide range of academic disciplines. This includes theology, especially in Jewish and Christian contexts, which has increasingly embraced core concepts of the philosopher such as "family resemblance," "language game," and "depth" and "surface grammar" in recent years. In Islamic theology, this reception has not occurred to the same extent, but initial approaches are now becoming observable.[10]

For this volume, Wittgenstein's conception of philosophy as a grammatical investigation is of central importance.[11] This approach underscores that theological discourse – like philosophy – can attain clarity only through an examination of language as it is used within religious practices, eschewing speculative abstractions. The main theme explored in this collection of articles revolves around the idea of "theology as grammar." By applying Wittgenstein's methodology, one can delve beyond the superficial grammar of religious expressions and uncover their underlying grammatical arrangement. This approach illuminates the tensions and intricacies inherent in theological discussions, particularly those related to language that pertains to the divine. At the same time, this book is also committed

---

9 For an overview of his biography see Grayling, Anthony Clifford, *Wittgenstein: A Very Short Introduction*, Oxford: Oxford University Press, 2001, 1–15; Biletzki, Anat/Matar, Anat, "Ludwig Wittgenstein," published online in: Edward N. Zalta (ed.), The Stanford Encyclopedia of Philosophy, originally published in 2002, substantially revised in 2021, https://plato.stanford.edu/archives/win2021/entries/wittgenstein/ (accessed on 10.01.2024); Schulte, Joachim, *Wittgenstein. Eine Einführung*, Stuttgart: Reclam, 2016, 9–25.

10 At Paderborn university, two PhD projects currently focus on Wittgenstein and Islamic theology, see: https://kw.uni-paderborn.de/institut-fuer-katholische-theologie/systematische-theologie/forschung/komparative-theologie-und-islam (accessed on 10.01.2024).

11 As an introduction to Wittgenstein and religious belief see Schönbaumsfeld, Genia, *Wittgenstein on Religious Belief*, Cambridge: Cambridge University Press, 2023.

to an interreligious perspective, bringing together Jewish, Christian, and Muslim insights into the concept of God. This is done by focussing on a number of selected questions originating from the three religious traditions.

This volume has several target audiences: primarily, philosophers of religion and theologians from the three religions, as well as researchers engaged in inter-religious studies. Additionally, it is also addressed to individuals in society. Given that the chosen approach aims to examine the grammar of key concepts in the context of their significance for the lives of believers, it should also have practical relevance. In this sense, a bridge is intended to be built from academic theology to society.

The book is the product of the research project *Wittgenstein and Theology: An Approach to the Grammar of the Word 'God' in the Abrahamic Religions*, which was made possible by the *Academy for Islam in Research and Society* (AIWG) in the form of a Reading Weekend in 2020. Building on Ludwig Wittgenstein's in-sights into the nature of language, the project had the aim to examine to what extent the meaning of religious expressions can be situated in lived, context-dependent language practices. Using the word "God" as an example, the approach aimed to facilitate interreligious dialogue between Judaism, Christianity, and Islam. The project involved a Reading Weekend where key passages from Witt-genstein's work were discussed with a group of scholars from Islamic theological studies and related disciplines from Germany and other countries. Additionally, in December 2021, a workshop was held at the *Bavarian Research Center for Inter-religious Discourses* (BaFID), during which the initial drafts of the contributions gathered in this volume were presented and discussed. This also allowed for the inclusion of this book in the series *Key Concepts in Interreligious Discourses* (KCID), edited by Georges Tamer.

The edited book is structured as follows: The main body comprises of three distinct studies from the different religions, with the first contribution by Genia Schönbaumsfeld providing a general overview of various relevant elements of Wittgenstein's philosophy. She then explores its significance for central Christian beliefs. The second contribution is Daniel Weiss' examination of the Jewish con-ception of the name of God, followed by Farid Suleiman's study of the implica-tions of Wittgenstein's approaches for Islamic theology. After the main section of the book, an epilogue follows in which the three authors of the studies refer to each other and offer reflections on the other contributions, but in reverse order.

Genia Schönbaumsfeld's contribution *"An Equation Entirely Unlike Any of the Familiar Curves": Wittgenstein on the Grammar of "God," the Trinity, and the Meaning of Religious Language* begins by introducing relevant themes of Wittgen-stein's later philosophy. According to this approach, many philosophical problems arise from conceptual confusion and can only be dissolved by re-examining our use of words. According to Schönbaumsfeld, Wittgenstein calls for abandoning the idea that the essence of language lies in naming objects (the "Augustinian picture of language") and instead focuses on the complex roles which words play within language-games or linguistic practices. Applying this to the concept of God, Wittgenstein argues that mistaking grammatical features of a concept for empirical ones leads to confusion and nonsensical questions. This can be seen in the example of the Trinity: Talking about God as a human being results in asking ridiculous and perhaps even blasphemous questions. Wittgenstein suggests that the grammar of "God" includes aspects of human grammar, such as talking about God "hearing" and "seeing", alongside elements that are entirely dissimilar to human beings. A fully developed understanding of religious concepts requires considering their role in the believer's life and religious practice. Otherwise, Schönbaumsfeld argues in interpreting Wittgenstein, one is in danger of reducing religious language to absurd ideas, very much like misunderstanding the mathematical equation of a new curve as a random combination of familiar elements.

Daniel H. Weiss explores in his article *Wittgenstein and the Rabbinic Grammar of God's Name* the theological implications of ascribing a specific name to God by conducting a Wittgenstein-inspired analysis of classical rabbinic literature and modern Jewish philosophy of religion. According to the Hebrew Bible, God has a specific proper name (*YHVH*), but humans are told to avoid wrongful use of it. Weiss contrasts this with the view held by some Christian and Jewish traditions, suggesting that God, as the "creator of all," should be regarded as nameless or "beyond names." The classical rabbinic sources, however, retain the idea of God's name while discussing its usage restrictions, differentiating between its pronunciation (*YHVH*) in the Temple and its substitute term (*Adonai*) outside the Temple. This pattern is analyzed as the "grammar" of God's name. To address objections related to anthropomorphism, Weiss introduces Wittgenstein's methodology of "looking" rather than merely "thinking," which reveals that the assumption of God's name implying a created being may be unnecessary. The rabbinic approach, in alignment with Wittgenstein's "grammatical" orientation, upholds the notion of God's name while maintaining respect and transcendence befitting the creator. This contribution demonstrates how Wittgenstein's approach can liberate theologians and philosophers from undue concerns surrounding the concept of God's name.

In Farid Suleiman's paper *The Grammar of "God" – Muslim Perspectives*, the distinction between the "God of the philosophers" and the "God of Abraham" is explored, and "Theology as Grammar" is applied as a therapeutic solution to the question of God's goodness. The "God of the philosophers" refers to a specific concept of God, influenced by Plato and prevalent in Western and Islamic philosophical traditions. It constructs a logical theory about God and is significant in analytic philosophy of religion. It was this approach which led Fakhr ad-Dīn ar-

Rāzī (d. 1210/606) to consider the notion of God's goodness as unintelligible. In this context, Suleiman suggests utilizing Wittgenstein's ideas to employ "Theology as Grammar" as a solution for resolving the philosophical confusion that emerges from misconceptions about language. For instance, philosophers often try to assess God's goodness using the same criteria as human goodness. A non-confused understanding of God's goodness, however, can be achieved by recognizing the limitations of language and the context-dependent nature of meaning. The statement "God is good" should be seen as a regulative picture with meaningful application in an Islamic way of life, rather than a proposition contingent on empirical facts. In this sense, the Qur'ān can be seen as a collection of religious pictures that shape Islamic belief, enabling believers to establish meaningful connections between the creator and creation through religious practice. By interpreting the Qur'ān in this manner, theology can return to the "God of Abraham".

Overall, it can be said that the proposed approach has proven to be highly fruitful. The various essays are connected through Wittgenstein's method of grammatical investigation. In fact, different aspects of its application can be observed in the three studies: For instance, Suleiman demonstrates how pre-modern Muslim thinkers like ar-Rāzī encountered precisely the difficulties that Wittgenstein describes as "when language goes on holiday," while Weiss, on the other hand, shows how the thought of the rabbis in Late Antiquity can be better understood and more appreciated if investigated through a grammatical approach. Schönbaumsfeld takes her inspiration from Wittgenstein's own (though very few) comments on theology in order to develop an adequate understanding of religious concepts. Considering the specific conditions in the three religious traditions, the essays collectively lead to a better understanding of how Wittgenstein's later philosophy can positively enrich the practice of theology, while the doctrinal differences recede into the background.

While the present volume yields promising findings, it is important to acknowledge the inherent limitations within the scope of the studies. Although the examination of the grammar of "God" delves into what may be deemed the quintessential concept of theology, it remains both conceivable and highly desirable to explore additional concepts. This endeavor could commence with Judaism, Christianity and Islam and, subsequently, broaden its scope to encompass a broader range of religions. By undertaking such comprehensive investigations, we will be able to elucidate the possibilities and constraints of a Wittgenstein-inspired approach within the realm of theology.

At the same time, this approach – which takes its departure point from a "figure of the third" taken from our modern context – should not be understood as a rejection of engaging with the shared historical and intertwined influences on the three theologies. In fact, inter-theological entanglements present a compelling reality worthy of exploration and discussion. Alongside the common reception of Greek philosophy, the shared biblical heritage serves as an important connecting element. The historical exchange processes between the theologies can serve as a significant starting point for further reflections, which should be given even greater attention in the future.[12] The collective engagement with Wittgenstein, as seen in this volume, rather demonstrates that shared challenges – including those arising from shared tradition(s) – strongly advocate for experimenting with common strategies for solutions. This, in the best sense, can lead to learning from one another.

Bibliography

Bauer, Jochen, *Religionsunterricht für alle. Eine multitheologische Fachdidaktik*, Stuttgart: Kohlhammer, 2019.

Bernhardt, Reinhold, *Inter-Religio. Das Christentum in Beziehung zu anderen Religionen*, Zürich: TVZ, 2019.

Biletzki, Anat/Matar, Anat, "Ludwig Wittgenstein," published online in: Edward N. Zalta (ed.), *The Stanford Encyclopedia of Philosophy*, originally published in 2002, substantially revised in 2021, https://plato.stanford.edu/archives/win2021/entries/wittgenstein/ (accessed on 10.01.2024).

Dobbelaere, Karel, "The Meaning and Scope of Secularization," in: Peter B. Clarke (ed.), *The Oxford Handbook of the Sociology of Religion*, 599–615, Oxford: Oxford University Press, 2009.

Eßlinger, Eva et al. (eds.), *Die Figur des Dritten. Ein kulturwissenschaftliches Paradigma*, Frankfurt am Main: Suhrkamp, 2010.

Grayling, Anthony Clifford, *Wittgenstein: A Very Short Introduction*, Oxford: Oxford University Press, 2001.

Krochmalnik, Daniel, "Trialog 'in unserer Zeit' (Nostra Aetate). Ein Beitrag zum Weiterdenken der Konzilserklärung," in: Reinhold Boschki/ Josef Wohlmuth (eds.), *Nostra Aetate 4*, 207–214, Leiden: Brill/Schöningh, 2015.

Liedhegener, Antonius, "Pluralisierung," in: Detlef Pollack et al. (eds.), *Handbuch Religionssoziologie*, 347–382, Wiesbaden: Springer VS, 2018.

Pollack, Detlef, "Säkularisierung," in: Detlef Pollack et al. (eds.), *Handbuch Religionssoziologie*, 303–327, Wiesbaden: Springer VS, 2018.

Schönbaumsfeld, Genia, *Wittgenstein on Religious Belief*, Cambridge: Cambridge University Press, 2023.

Schulte, Joachim, *Wittgenstein. Eine Einführung*, Stuttgart: Reclam, 2016.

Sievers, Mira/Tobias Specker, "Intertheologie: Jenseits von Gemeinsamkeiten und Unterschieden," *Wort und Antwort* 62 (2021), 167–173.

---

12 Such an approach focusing on the theological exchange traditions between the monotheistic religions can be described as "inter-theology", see: Sievers, Mira/Tobias Specker, "Intertheologie: Jenseits von Gemeinsamkeiten und Unterschieden," *Wort und Antwort* 62 (2021), 167–173.

Silk, Mark, "The Abrahamic Religions as a Modern Concept," in: Adam J. Silverstein/Guy G. Stroumsa (eds.), *The Oxford Handbook of the Abrahamic Religions*, 71–87, Oxford: Oxford University Press, 2005.

Stackhouse, John G., "Religious Diversity, Secularization, and Postmodernity," in: Chad Meister (ed.), *The Oxford Handbook of Religious Diversity*, 239–249, Oxford: Oxford University Press, 2010.

Wissenschaftsrat (ed.), *Empfehlungen zur Weiterentwicklung von Theologien und religionsbezogenen Wissenschaften an deutschen Hochschulen*, Berlin/Köln, 2010, http://www.wissenschaftsrat.de/download/archiv/9678-10.html (accessed on 10.01.2024).

Suggestions for Further Reading

Schönbaumsfeld, Genia, *Wittgenstein on Religious Belief*, Cambridge: Cambridge University Press, 2023.

Sievers, Mira/Tobias Specker, "Intertheologie: Jenseits von Gemeinsamkeiten und Unterschieden," *Wort und Antwort* 62 (2021), 167–173.

Von Stosch, Klaus, "Wittgenstein's Later Philosophy as Foundation of Comparative Theology," in: Gorazd Andrejč/Daniel H. Weiss (eds.), *Interpreting Interreligious Relations with Wittgenstein: Philosophy, Theology and Religious Studies*, 73–96, Leiden/Boston: Brill, 2019.

Genia Schönbaumsfeld

"An Equation Entirely Unlike Any of the Familiar Curves": Wittgenstein on the Grammar of "God," the Trinity, and the Meaning of Religious Language

1 Introduction

Although there is little overt discussion of religious themes in Wittgenstein's magnum opus, *Philosophical Investigations*, Wittgenstein's later philosophy has significant implications for understanding religious belief and language. A fuller picture emerges, if what is said in the latter work is supplemented by additional material gleaned from Wittgenstein's various Cambridge lectures, his conversations with Rush Rhees, and the collection of remarks known as *Culture and Value* (CV henceforth). This material shows not only that religious questions were of the first importance to Wittgenstein, it also reveals that he grappled with these questions in a manner reminiscent of his general approach to philosophical problems. That is to say, in both philosophy and religion, Wittgenstein eschews metaphysical theorizing in favour of gaining clarity through the method of a grammatical investigation of our concepts.

In this essay, I will start by giving a general overview of some relevant themes from Wittgenstein's later philosophy before moving on to an in-depth examination of what a grammatical investigation of the concept of "God" involves, and what problems it enables us to dissolve. I will then move on to a consideration of what implications Wittgenstein's conception has for an understanding of the meaning of religious language. By way of concluding, I briefly consider and respond to a common objection.

2 Themes from Wittgenstein's Later Philosophy

Wittgenstein dedicated his life to the pursuit of clarity – both within philosophy itself as well as in respect of himself. The following remark from *Philosophical Investigations* (PI henceforth) serves to bring this out: "We don't want to refine or complete the system of rules for the use of our words in unheard-of ways. For the clarity that we are aiming at is indeed *complete* clarity. But this simply means that the philosophical problems should *completely* disappear" (PI §133).

https://doi.org/10.1515/9783111501611-002

It is one of the most distinctive features of Wittgenstein's later philosophy that he believes that it is impossible to *solve* philosophical problems, as these are spawned by conceptual confusion and illusion. Rather, these problems can only be *dissolved* by putting together what we have always known, but have somehow lost sight of. In other words, philosophy is not a body of knowledge for Wittgenstein, consisting of a set of metaphysical truths, but rather the *activity* of logical (grammatical/conceptual) clarification or elucidation[1]. As Wittgenstein says: "A main source of our failure to understand is that we don't have *an overview* of the use of our words. – Our grammar is deficient in surveyability. A surveyable representation produces precisely that kind of understanding which consists in 'seeing connections'" (PI §122).

The particular form our language takes can mislead us. The most basic misconception that Wittgenstein identifies in this respect – one that gives rise to a whole host of philosophical difficulties and misbegotten theories – is the temptation to think that "where our language suggests a body and there is none: there, we should like to say, is a *spirit* (*Geist*)" (PI §36). In other words, because our language is full of substantives, and we naively assume that the meaning of a word is the object it refers to – Wittgenstein calls this the "Augustinian" picture of language, as it is by no means peculiar only to philosophy – if we are unable actually to find such an object in the world, we take it that there must be a "supernatural" object or spirit that the word can refer to instead. Arguably, this was behind Plato's theory of the Forms – the "Form of the Good" or of "Beauty" can never be found in the myriad different objects we apply the words "good" or "beautiful" to, but only in a metaphysical realm of "Forms" populated by the abstract objects that are allegedly the referents of these unadulterated essences. Similarly, mathematicians (including philosophers of mathematics) think that since number words cannot refer to empirical objects in the world, they must refer instead to abstract objects. Contemporary metaphysicians, on the other hand, believe that propositions, properties and "truth-makers" are abstract objects to be investigated and theorized about. Last, but not least, philosophers of religion, theologians and ordinary religious people think that the word "God" is the name of a supernatural object or entity.

The arguments in favour of these assumptions are often surprisingly thin, but we do not notice this, because it seems to us that things *must* be the way the Augustinian picture suggests. That is to say, we are primarily taken in by the fact that words like "beauty," "proposition," "one," "God," appear to operate in

---

1 This was a view that Wittgenstein already held in the *Tractatus* and that he never changed his mind on, despite his later conception of philosophy being in many respects very different from his earlier one. In this essay, I will mainly confine myself to discussing Wittgenstein's later philosophy and its implications for the understanding of religious belief.

exactly the same way as more ordinary words whose referents we can straight-forwardly point to: "cat," "table," "chair." From this we go on to draw the conclusion that in the former case, too, there must be objects these words stand for, it's just that they are not empirically locatable. In other words, we are taken in by the "surface grammar" of our words – how our words appear to function linguistically in a sentence – even though this may not be a good guide to what is really going on. Wittgenstein explains:

> In the use of words, one might distinguish "surface grammar" from "depth grammar." What immediately impresses itself upon us about the use of a word is the way it is used in the sentence structure, the part of its use – one might say – that can be taken in by the ear. – And now compare the depth grammar, say of the verb "to mean," with what its surface grammar would lead us to presume. No wonder one finds it difficult to know one's way about (PI §664).

The surface grammar of the verb "to mean" suggests that it's the name of a mental process going on in the hidden medium of "the mind" (another substantive we mistake for the name of an entity), whereas Wittgenstein's investigation shows that its depth grammar is actually quite different. Rather than referring to a hidden process, "to mean" is much more similar to "to be able to do something": A competent language-user can mean "X" rather than "Y," not because something special goes on in their mind (or brain), but because they are generally able to apply the words "X" and "Y" with facility. Whether a speaker meant "X" or "Y" can, therefore, be determined, not by looking into the speaker's mind, but by ascertaining whether the speaker has mastered a particular technique, what the speaker goes on to say and do, what consequences the speaker would be prepared (or not prepared) to draw etc.

So, when Wittgenstein says, at PI §122, that our grammar is deficient in surveyability, what he means is that the "depth grammar" is still unclear to us. All we see is the surface grammar, the mere syntactical structure of the word or sentence – "the use that can be taken in by the ear" – not the actual use, what early Wittgenstein would have called the "logical syntax" of the sign: the rules for the correct use of the word, which can be hidden underneath the word's apparent use (the "surface grammar") in the way that the real form of a body may be obscured by a person's clothes.

Attending to the "depth grammar," however, requires a willingness to look beyond the surface; to refuse to be taken in by superficial linguistic appearances that may lead one astray. This is difficult, as the surface appearance may be attractive and tempt us to want to continue to view the problem in the accustomed manner. For this reason, Wittgenstein thinks that the struggle for clarity requires both an intellectual effort, as well as an engagement of the will. We need the intellectual acumen to see through the deceptive appearances, but also require the will-power to resist the spell that language casts: "A *picture* held us captive. And we couldn't get outside it, for it lay in our language, and language only seemed to repeat it to us inexorably" (PI §115).

The Augustinian picture seems natural and intuitive, as it reduces the diversity of the actual function of words to an easily graspable common denominator: "the words in language name objects – sentences are combinations of such names" (PI §1). Wittgenstein himself was tempted by something like such a view in his early work, the *Tractatus*. Later Wittgenstein realizes, however, that language is not as uniform as the Augustinian picture would have us believe. There are many different kinds of words and they do not all function as names: "Someone who describes the learning of language in this way [by ostensive definition] is, I believe, thinking primarily of nouns like 'table', 'chair', 'bread', and of people's names, and only secondarily of the names of certain actions and properties; and of the remaining kinds of word as something that will take care of itself" (PI §1). Naturally, the remaining kinds of word do *not* take care of themselves, which is why philosophers need to invent abstract entities in order to explain how these words can function like names at all.

Rather than trying to press the diversity of the functions of words into a uniform mould that distorts them, however, Wittgenstein suggests that we would do better to abandon our preconceived idea that the essence of language consists in naming. For this would enable us to see that the role that a word plays in language is complex and cannot be reduced to a "one size fits all." "Think just of exclamations," Wittgenstein says, "with their completely different functions. Water! Away! Ow! Help! Splendid! No! Are you still inclined to call these words 'names of objects'?"(PI §27).

Whether a word functions as the name of an object – and Wittgenstein does not deny that some words are names[2] – is not something that can be settled independently of attending to the context in which the word is used. It is the overall role the word plays in the language-game or linguistic practice that tells us what kind of word it is and what it does. This is why Wittgenstein says: "For a *large* class of cases of the employment of the word 'meaning' – though not for *all* – this word can be explained in this way: the meaning of a word is its use in the language" (PI §43). Just as the significance of the different chess pieces can be explained by describing the moves these pieces can make in the game of chess, so

---

2 Neither does he deny that (some) words refer to objects. What he does deny is that the meaning is something independent of the word that can be reified (either an empirical or an abstract object).

the significance of a word can be explained by looking at how the word is employed in a particular language-game. This is not to advance a new theory of meaning – hence the warning that Wittgenstein's suggestion is not meant to apply across the board – but to give us the tools to free ourselves from enslavement to the Augustinian picture that made us believe that there is only one way that things can be.

3 The Grammar of "God"

Let us now apply the lessons learnt in the previous section to an understanding of religious belief. In PI themselves there is only one (famous) remark about theology: "Grammar tells what kind of object anything is (Theology as grammar.)" (PI §372).

Wittgenstein believes that one of the main confusions that arise in philosophy (and elsewhere) is to mistake a grammatical (logical) feature of a concept for an empirical one and to end up predicating of the thing what lies in the mode of representation (PI §104). The comparison with theology and the concept of "God" serves to make this perspicuous (which is perhaps why theology is the first thing that occurs to Wittgenstein in this regard). A passage from the recently published lectures from the early 1930's throws more light on what Wittgenstein might have in mind here: "Now (a) suppose 'god' means something like a human being; then 'he has 2 arms' & 'he has 4 arms' are not grammatical propositions but (b) suppose someone says: You can't talk of god having arms, this is grammatical."[3]

If we think the word "God" is the name of something very akin to a human being, then saying that this god has two or four arms would not be different from offering a straightforward empirical description of something, e.g. "this animal has two legs" or "this animal has four legs." Here we are describing something contingent that could be otherwise, had the world been different in some way. But if we say something like: "It makes no sense to speak of God having arms," then we are making a grammatical remark that shows that it is part of the concept of God that we can't attribute certain physical features to him – it's not that God is an entity who just happens not to have these characteristics.

The essential features of our concepts are specified by the grammar of the concept. To give a non-theological example, to say that "one is a number" is not to attribute some predicate (that of numberhood) to an abstract object, but to tell us

---

3 Wittgenstein, Ludwig, *Lectures. Cambridge 1930–33*, ed. David Stern/Brian Rogers/Gabriel Citron, New York: Cambridge University Press, 2016, 321.

how the word "one" functions in our language – namely, as a number-word. To say that "red is a colour" is similarly to say something about the grammar of "red," not to give a description of an esoteric object. To think otherwise, is precisely to predicate of the thing what lies in the mode of representation: to believe one is tracing the thing's nature when in fact you are giving a rule for the correct use of a word (i.e. something grammatical).

Many philosophical and theological problems arise if one doesn't heed this distinction. In an illuminating conversation with Rush Rhees, Wittgenstein says:

> Our statements about God have a different grammar from our statements about human beings. And if you try to talk about God as you would talk about a human being, you are likely to come to talk nonsense, to ask nonsensical questions and so on. In talking about God we often use images or parts of images that apply to human beings. This is so when we say: "Wherever you are, God always sees what you do." We know how this statement is used, and that is all right.
>
> So we may speak also of God's hearing our prayers. You might say then that in our picture of God there are eyes and ears. But it makes no sense if you then try to fill in the picture and think of God as having teeth and eyelashes and stomach and tendons and toenails. So we might say that our picture of God is like a picture of a human being with holes in it. Which means that the grammar of our language about God has holes in it if you look at it as the grammar of statements about a human being.
>
> In describing our picture of God we may speak of it as being made up of parts of a picture of a human being together with other things which have no resemblance to any part of a human being. You might start the description of a curve by taking drawings of familiar curves: a circle, an ellipse, a parabola, a hyperbola. Then describe it by saying: "You see here it is part of a parabola, there then it is part of a circle, here it is a straight line which goes into part of a spiral, etc." And the curve you described might then have an equation entirely unlike any of the familiar curves.[4]

Unpacking Wittgenstein's line of reasoning, this passage seems to contain the following dialectical progression:
(1) If you try to talk about God as you would about a human being, you are likely to speak nonsense (ask nonsensical questions etc.).
(2) In talking about God, we nevertheless use images or parts of images derived from ordinary talk about human beings (e.g. "Wherever you are, God always sees what you do").
(3) These similarities may obscure the grammatical differences between "God-talk" and ordinary "human being" language.

---

4 Rhees, Rush, "On Religion: Notes on Four Conversations with Wittgenstein," *Faith and Philosophy: Journal of the Society of Christian Philosophers* 18, no. 4 (2001), 403.

(4) If so, (3) may either lead us back to (1) and the conclusion that the "grammar of our language about God has holes in it," or we come to realize that the similarities notwithstanding, we actually have "an equation entirely unlike any of the familiar curves."

In what follows, I will try to elucidate what (1)–(4) imply and how Wittgenstein's contention that, in respect to our picture of God, we have "an equation entirely unlike any of the familiar curves" can be understood.

Let's start with the question: Why would one speak nonsense if one were to talk about God as one would about a human being? Primarily, Wittgenstein seems to think, because one would end up saying all sorts of ridiculous and blasphemous things. The clearly ridiculous things would be asking questions such as, "Does God have toenails? Does God have a stomach?" Such questions sound ridiculous (and blasphemous), because they betray a category mistake: God is not a "gaseous vertebrate"[5] with invisible stomach and toenails.

Furthermore, such an anthropomorphic conception of God (God as invisible super-human) would raise a whole host of other issues. That is to say, if human grammar were the right grammar for "God," it would make sense to ask the following further questions: "Where does God live? Is it possible to find his home? Is God bored?" etcetera. On such a conception, the monotheistic God would not differ very much from the Greek Gods who live on Mount Olympus and get into the kind of scrapes human beings would also easily get into.

Now one might think that, apart from the militant atheists, who believe that people engage in religious practices out of sheer stupidity, there are not many Christian theologians or religious believers who would be happy to ascribe such a crude grammar to the word "God." But such an appearance would be deceptive, as quite often, an anthropomorphic conception of God comes dressed in metaphysical garb, which can make the crudeness harder to spot. For example, the God of analytic theism is conceived as an all-powerful, all-knowing, all-good "person without a body" – where a "person without a body" is usually regarded in Cartesian manner as a purely "mental substance"[6]. Here the idea is that human beings have both a mind and a body – where, if you are a Cartesian (or neo-Cartesian), these words refer to distinct substances (or entities). Hence, if God is like a person, but lacks a body, he comes out, on this view, as being a super-

---

5 The phrase is Ernst Häckel's and mentioned by Wittgenstein in the *Cambridge Lectures*.
6 See, for example, Swinburne, Richard, "Philosophical Theism," in: D. Z. Phillips/Timothy Tessin (eds.), *Philosophy of Religion in the 21st Century*, 1–20, New York: Palgrave, 2001; Swinburne, Richard, *The Coherence of Theism*, Oxford: Oxford University Press, 2016.

powerful "mental substance." This shows that the God of analytic theism is a "gaseous vertebrate."

Quite apart from all the other problems that such a conception raises[7], the "gaseous vertebrate" view is clearly driven by the Augustinian picture of language: the meaning of a word is the object it stands for. "God," being a proper name, i.e. the name of a person – but obviously not of a physical one with tendons and toenails – must, therefore, be the name of a disembodied one: a purely "spiritual" being ("where our language suggests a body and there is none: there, we should like to say, is a *spirit* (*Geist*)" (PI §36)). In other words, the "surface grammar" of the word "God" tempts us to think that "God" names a human-like object, when, really, Wittgenstein is suggesting, the "depth grammar" is quite different.

But how do we work out what the depth grammar is? In the same way as we would with any other word: by attending to its overall use in the language or practice. Wittgenstein says:

> Really what I should like to say is that here too what is important is not the *words* you use or what you think while saying them, so much as the difference that they make at different points in your life. How do I know that two people mean the same when each says he believes in God? And just the same thing goes for the Trinity. Theology that insists on *certain* words & phrases & prohibits others, makes nothing clearer. (Karl Barth)

> It gesticulates with words, as it were, because it wants to say something & does not know how to express it. *Practice* gives the words their sense (CV 97/85[8]).

What Wittgenstein seems to be saying here is that it is not possible to find out what someone means – or, indeed, whether two people mean the same – merely by looking at the words these people use. For they can use the *same words* and yet mean something completely different. The Augustinian picture glosses over this important insight by insisting that all that matters to meaning is reference: as long as we have some idea of what the objects are that the words in question are supposed to refer to, we know what the words mean. But this, of course, is very simplistic. Not only is "reference" itself a word in the language, which might not

---

7 For further discussion, see Schönbaumsfeld, Genia, *A Confusion of the Spheres: Kierkegaard and Wittgenstein on Philosophy and Religion*, Oxford: Oxford University Press, 2007; Schönbaumsfeld, Genia, "Ludwig Wittgenstein," in: Graham Oppy/Nick Trakakis (eds.), *History of Western Philosophy of Religion*, 61–74, Durham: Acumen, 2009; Schönbaumsfeld, Genia, "No Gaseous Vertebrates: Wittgenstein's Third Way," in: Duncan Pritchard/Nuno Venturinha (eds.), *Wittgenstein and the Epistemology of Religion*, Oxford: Oxford University Press, forthcoming.
8 The first number refers to the 1998 edition of CV, the second to the 1977 version; the translation is from the 1998 edition.

have a context-invariant use (i.e. "reference" might mean slightly different things in different contexts), but knowing only that the word stands for some object, does not give you the rules for the correct use of the word. This is why Wittgenstein spends so much time talking about ostensive definition at the beginning of PI. An ostensive definition will only teach me the use of a word, if the overall use of the word in the language is already clear (PI §30) – i.e. if I already know what a name is, for instance, and how it functions: "When one shows someone the king in chess and says 'This is the king', one does not thereby explain to him the use of this piece – unless he already knows the rules of the game except for this last point: the shape of the king" (PI §31).

I take it that when Wittgenstein mentions Karl Barth in the passage from CV 97/85, he is referring to Barth's conception of the Trinity (God Father, God Son and Holy Ghost) as "three ways of being" (*Seinsweisen*)[9]. Barth wanted to replace standard "three-personal" or "modal" conceptions of God – where God is regarded as manifesting himself either as three persons or as one person in different "modes" – with his own preferred version of *Seinsweisen*. Presumably, Wittgenstein is criticizing Barth for merely insisting on a different form of words, instead of clarifying the actual *use* of the word "Trinity." That is to say, Wittgenstein seems to think that banning one form of words, while allowing another, will not deepen my understanding of the relevant concept, unless the new form of words makes a significant difference to the religious practice itself. If it makes no difference which form of words is used, then these words are idle wheels: "a wheel that can be turned though nothing else moves with it is not part of the mechanism" (PI §271).

If, for example, I think that god is an invisible super-human with four arms, then this must, if it is to count as a genuine belief – rather than as an empty mouthing of words – have some implications for how I relate to this god and the rituals that I participate in. If, on the other hand, what I believe makes no difference to what I say and do, then this casts serious doubt on whether I really mean what I claim to mean. Wittgenstein's kindred spirit, the Danish philosopher, Søren Kierkegaard, is good on this point[10]. Kierkegaard spent most of his pseudonymous authorship trying to expose the "monstrous illusion"[11]: the false self-conception of the "Christians" in Christendom, who believe that being a Christian and being a good citizen are the same thing. These *soi-disant* Christians *thought*

---

9 Barth, Karl, *Church Dogmatics*, vol. 1, *The Doctrine of the Word of God*, ed. G. W. Bromiley/ T. F. Torrance, London/New York: T&T Clark, 2003, 355.
10 For an in-depth study of the similarities between Kierkegaard and Wittgenstein, see Schönbaumsfeld, *A Confusion of the Spheres*.
11 Kierkegaard, Søren, *The Point of View*, ed. and trans. Howard and Edna Hong, Princeton: Princeton University Press, 1998, 43.

they were Christian, and professed to be Christian, even though their *lives* were, in fact, very far removed from Christ's teachings.

Now, one can whole-heartedly endorse these points, but nevertheless wonder whether Wittgenstein's criticism of Barth is entirely fair. For regardless of what Barth's own, specific intentions were, one could read Barth's proposal in a more Wittgensteinian manner as an attempt to clarify the grammar of the concept "Trinity." That this would then not merely be an idle move, would manifest itself in a way similar to what Wittgenstein himself wants to achieve in philosophy: the vanishing of a problem and the loss of the desire to ask certain nonsensical questions.

Let me explain. Barth thought that talk of a "three person" God leads to the two standard (theological) ways of conceiving of the Trinity – "tritheism" and "modalism" – both of which he found extremely problematic. Tritheism, for example, makes people ask: How can one God be three distinct persons, and how is this compatible with the alleged monotheism of Christianity? Modalism, on the other hand, is the thought that God is not "triune" in and of Himself, but merely manifests Himself that way "in history." This, as Molnar notes, "leads to a search for a God behind the God who makes himself known as Father, Son, and Holy Spirit. Indeed, modalism not only posits a "hidden Fourth" behind the God who is eternally one and three, but for modalism, "the divine subjectivity is sucked up into the human subjectivity which enquires about a God that does not exist" (Barth, *Church Dogmatics* 1, 382).[12] In other words, modalism leads to a kind of regress problem, where we have to posit a fourth God "hidden" behind His "historical" manifestations, which might lead one to wonder whether there are further "Gods" behind the fourth and so on *ad infinitum.*

Of course, one might question whether this can really be the correct way of understanding talk of "personhood" in this context, and whether Barth, by making these criticisms, is not precisely exhibiting the confusion that Wittgenstein is trying to extirpate: that of being taken in by the surface grammar of the concept, instead of looking at how the "depth grammar" actually functions.[13] Indeed, this is presumably the reason why Wittgenstein is taking issue with Barth in the first place: "A theology which insists on the use of *certain particular* words and phrases, and outlaws others, does not make anything clearer." Nevertheless, I think it is possible to offer an interpretation of Barth's move that can avoid this objection. This may not be an interpretation that Barth himself would have en-

---

12 Molnar, Paul, "Barth on the Trinity," in: George Hunsinger/Keith Johnson (eds.), *The Wiley Blackwell Companion to Karl Barth: Barth and Dogmatics Volume 1*, 23–33, Oxford: Wiley Blackwell, 2020.

13 My thanks to Farid Suleiman for pressing me on this.

dorsed, but it allows us to read what Barth is doing in a way that is more consistent with Wittgenstein's conception.

My proposal is as follows. By introducing the concept of *"Seinsweisen,"* Barth is aiming to help someone, who is puzzled by the notion of a triune God. If our understanding of the concept (of the Trinity) is obstructed by the thought that "personhood" must imply either tritheism or modalism, then conceiving of "personhood" as a "way of being" might liberate us from having to draw these (nonsensical) conclusions. Naturally, this presupposes – and as Wittgenstein says – that we have a clearer grasp of what it means to speak of God's *Seinsweisen* than we do of talk of God's "three personhood"[14]. Whether this is the case, will depend on whether this new way of talking will cure our urge to ask the aforementioned problematic questions and save us from the bumps "that the understanding has got by running up against the limits of language. They – these bumps – make us see the value of that discovery" (PI §119). In this context, this might mean that Barth's conceptual clarification has enabled one to acquire a new way of thinking and speaking about God, which, in turn, allows one to participate in religious practices in a more whole-hearted way (as we will no longer be plagued by certain questions that call the practice itself into question).

In other words, the "surface grammar" of the concept of the Trinity might lead one to believe that the triune God is to be conceived analogously to three distinct human consciousnesses (or persons[15]) (with its incumbent problems), when the "depth grammar" is more fruitfully to be construed as operating along Barthian lines. On this interpretation, God's *"Seinsweisen"* are not to be reified into three different entities distinct from God Himself, just as the two different ways of seeing the duck-rabbit figure that Wittgenstein discusses in the second part of PI do not imply that the figure has two different natures corresponding to the two different ways of seeing it.

That is to say, just as we do not learn to see the rabbit-aspect of the duck-rabbit figure by discovering any additional, purely visual features of the duck-rabbit, so we don't come to believe in the triune God by making new discoveries about God's nature (namely, that He is really three). For, noticing an "aspect" – e.g. the rabbit-aspect in the duck-rabbit figure – is quite different from noticing an object's colour. While I can, for example, draw the object with or without this colour, and by doing so, show you what I have seen, I cannot, in the same way,

---

14 And I'm not going to try and adjudicate this theological debate here.
15 Whether it is a good idea to equate a person with an "individual self-consciousness" is not a question I can pursue here. I'm merely trying to give an interpretation of what Barth is doing that is maximally consistent with what I believe Wittgenstein is up to (whether or not Barth or Wittgenstein would have accepted this interpretation).

"show" you the rabbit-aspect, without simply reproducing the same lines (i.e., drawing the same thing). Rather, if asked what I now see, I would explain by "pointing to all sorts of pictures of rabbits, would perhaps have pointed to real rabbits, talked about their kind of life, or given an imitation of them" (PPF[16] §120).

So, one needs to go "beyond" the figure itself in order to explain what one sees, as the rabbit-aspect is not a property of the lines on the page in the same way that the shape of the "appendages" or the colour of the dot are distinct material properties of the object drawn. It is for this reason that Wittgenstein says that "seeing as" is not part of perception (PPF §137). Although in one sense, we "see" the drawing in a different way when we see the rabbit-aspect light up – which is why we continue to use the word "see" – in another sense we don't see anything different, because the arrangement of marks on the page hasn't changed. Consequently, what one is noticing is not an additional visual feature of the object, but rather "an internal relation between it and other objects" (PPF §248).

Learning to see internal relations between things, however, is not a matter of acquiring superior vision; it is much more akin to developing a new skill or conceptual capacity. This is why Wittgenstein says that "only of someone *capable* of making certain applications of the figure with facility would one say that he saw it now *this* way, now *that* way" (PPF §222). For example, someone who had never seen any rabbits – either in real life, picture books, or on the internet – would not be able to see the duck-rabbit as a rabbit. Neither would someone who had no experience with seeing two-dimensional pictures as representations of three-dimensional objects be able to see either the duck- or rabbit-aspect of the duck-rabbit figure. Instead, such a person would perhaps only be able to see what we see in an abstract drawing. Wittgenstein calls the inability to see "something as something" "aspect-blindness" (PPF §257). This is not a matter of having defective perceptual organs, but more akin to a lack of imagination or the absence of what, in another context, we call a "musical ear"[17].

If we apply these insights to the Barthian conception of the Trinity, the following picture emerges. Whereas before our conversion to Christianity (or before we developed, as Christians, a deeper understanding of the Trinity), we might have had some idea of what it means to speak of a belief in God, the notion that "God is three persons" would have seemed foreign and opaque to us. We would have failed to find a use for this picture of God; failed to apply it in our (religious) lives.

16 *Philosophy of Psychology* – A Fragment (formerly PI, part II).
17 For further discussion, see Schönbaumsfeld, Genia, "'Meaning-Dawning' in Wittgenstein's *Notebooks*: A Kierkegaardian Reading and Critique," *British Journal for the History of Philosophy* 26, vol. 3 (2018), 540–556, and Schönbaumsfeld, Genia, *Wittgenstein on Religious Belief*, Cambridge: Cambridge University Press, 2023.

As previously suggested, such a failure could have been compounded by the various intellectual problems that arise from standard ways of trying to understand the concept of the Trinity, which might have led one to dismiss it as a nonsensical notion. If, as a result of Barth's conceptual clarification, one now recognizes, however, that the grammar of a "triune" God should not be conceived along ordinary ways of thinking about human persons, then the way is paved for a "conceptual reorientation"[18] to occur. And such a conceptual reorientation, I submit, is like learning to see new aspects in things: Whereas before I could not see how God might appositely be describable as "triune," I am now able to recognize that the same God can be seen under three different aspects (Father, Son and Holy Ghost) – can be conceived as exhibiting three different "ways of being" – without this requiring any strange metaphysical contortions (tritheism or modalism). In this respect, I learn to see that there is an *internal* relation between the concept of God and the concept of the Trinity, not an external relation between three different entities that somehow need to be subsumed into a mereological sum.

4 Religious Language

The foregoing has important implications for how we should (or should not) understand religious language. Let's revisit what Wittgenstein says in the conversation with Rhees mentioned earlier:

> In describing our picture of God we may speak of it as being made up of parts of a picture of a human being together with other things which have no resemblance to any part of a human being. You might start the description of a curve by taking drawings of familiar curves: a circle, an ellipse, a parabola, a hyperbola. Then describe it by saying: "You see here it is part of a parabola, there then it is part of a circle, here it is a straight line which goes into part of a spiral, etc." And the curve you described might then have an equation entirely unlike any of the familiar curves.[19]

What Wittgenstein seems to be saying in this passage is that the grammar of "God" contains aspects of human grammar, such as talk of God "hearing" and "seeing," "together with other things which have no resemblance to any part of a human being." He then goes on to compare a description of this grammar to that of a very strange new curve, which also contains some familiar parts – e.g. parabola-parts,

---

18 See Diamond, Cora, "Wittgenstein on Religious Belief: The Gulfs Between Us," in: D. Z. Phillips/ Mario von der Ruhr (eds.), *Religion and Wittgenstein's Legacy*, 99–137, Aldershot: Ashgate, 2005.
19 Rhees, "On Religion," *Faith and Philosophy*, 403.

circular parts, parts of a spiral – while nevertheless having an equation which is "entirely unlike any of the familiar curves." The main point of this analogy, I would like to suggest, is to undermine an atomistic conception of meaning, according to which the meaning of a sentence is conceived as being nothing more than the sum-total of the meanings of the individual words comprising it (the sentence's "atoms"). Such a conception implies that if I understand the individual words of which a sentence is composed, I will automatically also understand the sentence as a whole. Although Wittgenstein has no sympathy for this view in any domain of discourse, it is particularly disastrous for the attempt to understand the meaning of religious language. A passage from Nielsen illustrates the problem:

> It is not (. . .) that I think that God is an object among objects, but I do think (. . .) that he must – in some very unclear sense – be taken to be a particular existent among existents though, of course, "the king" among existents, and a very special and mysterious existent, but not an object, not a kind of object, not just a categorical or classificatory notion, but not a non-particular either. Though he is said to be infinite, he is also said to be a person, and these two elements when put together seem at least to yield a glaringly incoherent notion. He cannot be an object – a spatio-temporal entity but he is also a he – a funny kind of he to be sure – who is also said to be a person – again a funny kind of person – who is taken to be a person without a body: a purely *spiritual* being. This makes him out to be a "peculiar reality" indeed. He gets to be even more peculiar when we are told he is an *infinite* person as well. But now language has really gone on a holiday.[20]

These remarks exemplify how the similarities and differences between God-talk and descriptions of ordinary human beings can confound us. On the one hand, God is said to be a person, which appears to make Him similar to a human being; on the other, He is described as "infinite," and, hence, as radically different from a human person. Small wonder that Nielsen ends up concluding that what we have here is a glaringly incoherent notion.

The way out of this quandary consists in heeding Wittgenstein's warning that, despite containing some familiar parts (words), the "equation" we are confronted with here is "entirely unlike any of the familiar curves." Consequently, we need to be wary of simply supposing, as does Nielsen, that there is nothing more to understanding the sentence "God is an infinite person" than by combining the individual atoms, "infinite" and "person," into a peculiar complex. What is more, we can also not just assume – and this is a further mistake that Nielsen makes – that it is possible to inspect the words alone, in order to find out whether they make sense or not. For this is to ignore Wittgenstein's important injunction that "practice gives the words their sense": that we cannot find out what words

---

20 Nielsen, Kai/Phillips, Dewi Zephaniah, *Wittgensteinian Fideism?*, London: SCM Press, 2005, 123.

and sentences mean without attending to the particular context of use in which these words have their life.

If we are, therefore, to have any hope of understanding what it means to call God infinite, we have to attend to the overall use to which this form of words is put in the religious practice as a whole. That is to say, we cannot just assume that because we know what "person" and "infinite" mean in non-religious contexts, we consequently know what it means to say these things about God – just as knowing what "person" and "three" mean in ordinary contexts will not automatically help one to understand what it means to speak of a "triune" God (indeed, and as we have already seen, it may mislead one into believing that the concept of the Trinity implies that three distinct entities are really one and the same).

For, as Wittgenstein already realized in the *Tractatus*, a *Satz* is more than the aggregation of its individual parts: "Only propositions have sense; only in the nexus (*Zusammenhang*) of a proposition does a name have meaning" (TLP 3.3). In other words, the overall sense of the proposition contributes to the meaning of the individual parts (words). Consequently, sentence-meaning cannot be derived from a summation of the meanings of the individual parts (say, the meanings that a dictionary gives you). This implies that Nielsen is wrong to think that he should, straightforwardly, be able to understand God-talk, just because he is familiar with the individual words that the religious person uses to speak about God. For, as we have already seen in the previous section, the grammar of "God" – despite sharing features with ordinary descriptions of human beings – is really quite different from that of a human person (even a super-powerful one).

But Nielsen makes a further mistake, not unconnected to the previous ones: He assumes that the prime function of religious language is to convey information about God. It is doubtful, however, whether the religious believer wants to inform anyone of a state of affairs, when he says that God is infinite. Rather, this form of words should be regarded as being more akin to a profession of faith than to a straightforward description.[21] Later Wittgenstein is good on the distinction between sentences having a merely instrumental use (where that use is primarily to convey information of some sort), and sentences being, as it were, ends in themselves:

> If we compare a proposition to a picture [as Wittgenstein did in the *Tractatus*], we must consider whether we are comparing it to a portrait (a historical representation) or to a genre-picture. And both comparisons make sense.

---

[21] D.Z. Phillips was one of the first philosophers to make this clear. See, for example, Phillips, Dewi Zephaniah, *The Concept of Prayer*, London: Routledge, 2015.

> When I look at a genre-picture, it "tells" me something, even though I don't believe (imagine) for a moment that the people I see in it really exist, or that there have really been people in that situation. For suppose I ask, "*What* does it tell me, then?" (PI §522)

> "A picture tells me itself" is what I'd like to say. That is, its telling me something consists in its own structure, in *its* own form and colours (PI §523).

In these passages, Wittgenstein seems to be identifying two ways in which a sentence can "tell" me something: either by straightforwardly conveying information about a particular state of affairs – where this information could also be conveyed by some other means (or by using a different sentence that expresses the same thought) – or by "telling me something" in a way that is not specifiable independently of using the precise form of words employed. In the first case, the thought expressed in the sentence could easily be paraphrased without loss; in the second case, the sentence in question could not easily be replaced by another which says the same. Wittgenstein clarifies:

> We speak of understanding a sentence in the sense in which it can be replaced by another which says the same; but also in the sense in which it cannot be replaced by any other. (Any more than one musical theme can be replaced by another.)

> In the one case, the thought in the sentence is what is common to different sentences; in the other, something that is expressed only by these words in these positions. (Understanding a poem.) (PI §531)

If the particular turn of phrase used is crucial to the kind of understanding sought – as, Wittgenstein is suggesting is the case in poetry and artistic language-use – then this implies that it is not sufficient to think that my understanding of such sentences can be displayed merely by being able to paraphrase the form of words in question. And if the same, as seems plausible, is the case for religious language-use, then Nielsen is rather rashly supposing that knowing what "infinite" means, say, in a mathematical context, is easily going to be transposable into a religious context. "Then has 'understanding' two different meanings here?" asks Wittgenstein, "No: I would rather say that these kinds of use of 'understanding' make up its meaning, make up my *concept* of understanding. For I *want* to apply the word 'understanding' to all this" (PI §532).

Following Wittgenstein's distinction, we can call the kind of understanding that consists only of being able to offer a passable paraphrase of the sentence in question "external" understanding, whereas the kind of understanding that consists of being able to see that the form of words in question is not instrumentally intersubstitutable, can be called "internal," to register the fact that what is grasped in the sentence is "internal" to this specific arrangement of words[22]. Applying this distinction to the passage from Nielsen, we can, therefore, say that Nielsen is missing the internal dimension of understanding when it comes to God-talk. Nielsen possesses an "external" understanding, in the sense that he knows what the relevant words mean in other contexts, and could, to this extent, offer some kind of paraphrase of "God is infinite," but he fails to see that these words might have a use that is not primarily informational or descriptive.

The fact that Nielsen fails to see this, is connected to his assumption that the whole sentence is no more than the sum of its parts. For an internal understanding that consists in recognizing how this particular form of words cannot be replaced by another which says the same, is antithetical to a conception that presupposes that sentence-meaning can be found through a process of "aggregation." So, to return to Wittgenstein's curve analogy, as long as one remains at the level of external understanding, all that one will see is that this strange curve seems to be a hodgepodge of incoherently put together parts: part parabola, part spiral and so forth. If, however, one recognizes that this curve has an equation quite different from all the familiar curves, then, instead of prioritizing what one believes are the familiar parts and attempting to aggregate them into a recalcitrant whole, one will start by focussing on the whole, in order to see how it (the whole) transforms the significance of its parts. This means not focussing on the whole in isolation – as it were in a vacuum – but in the context of the entire practice in which this whole plays a role.

In other words, it is not possible to explain the meaning of religious language merely by attempting to paraphrase it; by trying to distil out its informational content, as it were. For this, to use Cottingham's picturesque expression, is to employ a "fruit-juicer" method: to require "the clear liquid of a few propositions to be extracted for examination in isolation from what [one] take[s] to be the irrelevant pulpy mush of context."[23] And such a procedure, as Cottingham notes, does not give you the essence of a fruit, but only a not very palatable drink plus a pulpy mess.

We can now apply these insights to making sense of Wittgenstein's conversation with Rhees. At the beginning of the conversation quoted in the previous section, Wittgenstein says, "'Wherever you are, God always sees what you do.' We know how this statement is used, and that is all right." In other words, in respect

---

22 This terminology is Ridley's. Ridley, Aaron, *The Philosophy of Music: Theme and Variation*, Edinburgh: Edinburgh University Press, 2004, 32–33. I first made use of this distinction in Schönbaumsfeld, *A Confusion of the Spheres*, 182–183.
23 Cottingham, John, "Wittgenstein, Religion and Analytic Philosophy," in: Hans-Johann Glock/John Hyman (eds.), *Wittgenstein and Analytic Philosophy*, Oxford: Oxford University Press, 2009, 209.

to this particular way of talking about God, Wittgenstein seems to think that we would not get into confusion about the use of our words, perhaps because the phrase is so familiar to us and its meaning clearly metaphorical: It is not that God has strange sense-organs that are able to see all there is to be seen; rather, the phrase serves to remind one that God is always aware of what one is doing and judging one's actions (even if one manages to hide them from others). Or, to use another religious expression, God is omnipresent.

In respect to the latter phrase, however, Wittgenstein's confidence would potentially already be misplaced, for here one could easily imagine how surface grammar could trick us – namely, if we were to model the grammar of "omnipresent" on what it would be like for a human to be omnipresent; that is to say, simultaneously in all places at once. Naturally, if one construed the grammar thus, and hence offered a paraphrase of the sentence along these lines, then the statement would immediately strike one as incoherent and absurd, since it is necessarily impossible for an entity to be everywhere at the same time.

Arguably, Nielsen is making the same mistake, as he also appears to be modelling the grammar of God as "infinite person" on human grammar. God, on Nielsen's construction, is a type of *entity* that is describable as "infinite" – without limits; endless or everlasting – an idea that is, indeed, hard to make sense of if we think of something "bounded," such as a human person[24]. Had Nielsen proceeded more holistically, however, he might have realized that use of the word "infinite" seems precisely to signal that we cannot be speaking of something that one would ordinarily call an "entity" at all. This is why Wittgenstein says, "the way you use the word 'God' does not show *whom* you mean – but, rather, what you mean" (CV 58/ 50). And this is not a profession of atheism on Wittgenstein's part, but a grammatical remark that is supposed to alert us to the fact that the grammar of "God" does not function like the grammar of an entity or "person" in the ordinary sense.

The upshot of this is that it is only possible to develop an internal understanding of religious language-use, if one attends to the depth grammar of these expressions instead of being mesmerized by superficial similarities between God-talk and discourse about ordinary, empirical things. That is to say, although "in our picture of God there are eyes and ears," "it makes no sense if you then try to fill in the picture and think of God as having teeth and eyelashes and stomach and tendons and toenails."

In other words, when we speak of the "eye" of God or of God "hearing" our prayers, we are using these words in a different sense than in ordinary discourse where what we mean by "eye" is a physical sense-organ and by "hearing" we

---

24 It's not much easier to make sense of the notion if we think, instead, of an abstract object.

refer to a certain auditory process. Nevertheless, as Wittgenstein makes clear in PPF when talking about calling particular days of the week "fat" and "lean," it is precisely because the words have the ordinary meanings that they do, that we now want to employ them in this new way:

> Given the two concepts "fat" and "lean", would you be inclined to say that Wednesday was fat and Tuesday lean, or the other way round? (I am strongly inclined towards the former.) Now have "fat" and "lean" some different meaning here from their usual one? – They have a different use. – So ought I really to have used different words? Certainly not. – I want to use *these* words (with their familiar meanings) *here* (PPF §274).

> Asked "what do you really mean here by 'fat' and 'lean'?, I could only explain the meanings in the usual way. I could *not* point them out by using Tuesday and Wednesday as examples (PPF §275).

> Here one might speak of a "primary" and "secondary" meaning of a word. Only someone for whom the word has the former meaning uses it in the latter (PPF §276).

Something very interesting is going on in these passages. Despite Wittgenstein often being (erroneously) labelled a use-theorist of meaning, he is here saying that although "fat" and "lean" have a different *use* when applied to days of the week, he is hesitating to say that they have a different meaning. What is more, he emphasizes that he could only explain what "lean" and "fat" mean in this context in the ordinary way, which seems to imply that it is not possible to learn the new use merely by knowing what the words mean in ordinary contexts. Nevertheless, the new use is parasitic on the old use: only someone for whom the words have the old use, will be inclined to use the words in this novel way.

So, is what Wittgenstein calls "secondary sense" something like metaphorical meaning? Wittgenstein says "no": "If I say, 'For me the vowel e is yellow', I do not mean 'yellow' in a metaphorical meaning – for I could not express what I want to say in any other way than by means of the concept of yellow" (PIPF §278). Now, while one could challenge the thought that it is always necessary for something's being a metaphor that whatever it is that the metaphor is saying could also be expressed in another way, one can take Wittgenstein's point that what is essential to secondary sense is that I want to employ *these* words in *these* positions (compare PI §531). One cannot easily replace these words with something else.

It seems natural to connect the employment of words in a secondary sense with what Diamond calls a "conceptual reorientation." Such a reorientation occurs in situations where I am moved to employ old concepts in novel ways. Diamond gives the example of suddenly finding it apt to call George Eliot "beautiful" in despite of the fact that according to conventional criteria of beauty, Eliot is not a beautiful woman:

> She [George Eliot], that magnificently ugly woman, gives a totally transformed meaning to "beauty". Beauty itself becomes something entirely new for one, as one comes to see (to one's own amazement, perhaps) a powerful beauty residing in this woman (. . .). In such a case, she is not judged by a norm available through the concept of beauty; she shows the concept up, she moves one to use the words "beauty" and "beautiful" almost as new words, or as renewed words. She gives one a new vocabulary, a new way of taking the world in in one's words and of speaking about it to others.[25]

In this example, Diamond seems to be suggesting, George Eliot herself provides a new criterion for employment of the concept "beauty," rather than being judged by a norm made available through prior use of the concept. And something similar may happen in a religious context, when someone experiences a conversion and expresses this experience with the form of words: "God is infinite" or "God is omnipresent" (or "God is three").

Of course, there may be people who are unable to see how one could extend the concept of beauty to George Eliot, just as there are people who cannot see what it could mean to speak of God's infinitude or trinity. Not all potentially available secondary uses of concepts are equally available to everyone; just as certain aspects of the world can be perceived by some that others are blind to.

Fortunately, it is possible to work on oneself, in order to make new forms of seeing and understanding possible. This is why Wittgenstein says: "In religion it must be the case that corresponding to every level of devoutness there is a form of expression that has no sense at a lower level. For those still at the lower level this doctrine, which means something at the higher level, is null & void; it *can* only be understood *wrongly*, & so these words are *not* valid for such a person" (CV 37/32). In other words, the same form of expression can do different work for different people. What sense someone can make of an expression will, therefore, depend on the relative level of spiritual development of the person concerned. For instance, someone who thinks that Job's words, "the Lord has given, the Lord has taken away, blessed be the name of the Lord" is a cheap attempt at trying to justify the malevolent arbitrariness of the deity, is at a lower level of religious understanding than someone who sees it as an expression of one's trusting acceptance of God's sovereignty. Similarly, someone who believes that "God is three" is an incoherent metaphysical claim about a mereological entity, possesses less religious insight than someone who recognizes that it is an expression that shows that, for the Christian believer, "God Father," "Son" and "Holy Ghost" are three different ways of referring to the same God.

---

25 Diamond, *"Wittgenstein on Religious Belief,"* 125.

None of this is peculiar to the religious domain. In aesthetics, ethics and philosophy – in addition to music and other artistic endeavours – it is similarly true that one's understanding grows in proportion to how much one is able to develop certain relevant capacities: one's musicality, sensitivity, attention to detail, open-mindedness, altruism and so on. Why should it be any different in religion and the expectation be that whatever immediately meets the eye (or ear) must be sufficient to know what is meant? As we have already seen, the surface appearance may be extremely deceptive and embroil us in all sorts of confusions, if we are not vigilant.

Consequently, we must be careful that the familiar we recognize does not blind us to the unfamiliar we have yet to make sense of. Otherwise, instead of realizing that we are confronted by "an equation entirely unlike all familiar curves," we will rashly end up concluding that the grammar of God "has holes in it," or indeed, that it is, in Nielsen's words, "plain incoherent." Both responses can be avoided, if we look at the depth grammar and recognize that much religious discourse employs words in a secondary sense – a sense that can only be understood if we don't just inspect the words alone, but learn more about the religious practices in which these concepts have their life.

5 Conclusion: Just an Attitude?

By way of concluding, I will briefly address an objection[26] that might be looming at this point in the discussion. An apparently hard-nosed reader might want to say something like this: "If you are right that much religious language-use employs words in a secondary sense, is this not tantamount to saying that they are really used only to express an attitude?"[27] After all, Wittgenstein himself said the following:

It appears to me as though a religious belief could only be (something like) passionately committing oneself to a system of reference [of coordinates][28] [*Bezugssystem/Koordinaten-*

---

26 I have dealt with this objection extensively in other work (see, in particular, Schönbaumsfeld, *A Confusion of the Spheres* and Schönbaumsfeld, *Wittgenstein on Religious Belief*).

27 See, for example, Glock, Hans-Johann, *A Wittgenstein Dictionary*, Oxford: Blackwell, 1995 and Hyman, John, "The Gospel According to Wittgenstein," in: Mark Addis/Robert Arrington (eds.), *Wittgenstein and Philosophy of Religion*, 1–11, London: Routledge, 2001, for proponents of such an interpretation of Wittgenstein.

28 The 1998 edition has "system of coordinates," with "system of reference" as an alternative; the 1977 edition has "system of coordinates."

system]. Hence, although it's belief, it's really a way of living, or a way of judging [beurteilen] life. Passionately taking up *this* conception[29] [*Auffassung*] (CV 73/64).

Read the wrong way, this could make it sound like Wittgenstein is saying that Christianity requires commitment to a "doctrineless"[30] form of life, where all that matters is that you live a certain way, rather than that you hold certain kinds of belief.

Quite apart from all the other things wrong with such a reading of Wittgenstein, it should already be apparent from the discussion in previous sections that there can be no such thing as "grammar-free" doctrine for Wittgenstein. What the Christian doctrine amounts to – and, hence, what is involved in believing it – can, therefore, not be determined in a context-free manner by looking at the words alone. Consequently, Wittgenstein is not saying, in this passage or elsewhere, that the doctrine is irrelevant – or should be thrown out (he is not Don Cupitt[31] in disguise!) – rather, he is in the business of trying to elucidate precisely what the grammar of various credal points could amount to.

It is also worth emphasizing that in the passage cited above, Wittgenstein is not saying that religious belief is not *belief* (Glaube). Rather, he is saying that *although* it's belief, it's *also* a way of living. The original German makes this more evident than the not terribly good English translation that seems to oppose "belief" and "way of living" to each other, whereas the German reads: "Also obgleich es *Glaube* ist, doch eine Art des Lebens;" which carries the implication that religious belief is *both* belief *and* way of life.

That Wittgenstein should think that religious belief is simultaneously both of these things should, of course, not surprise us, given that he believes that "practice gives the words their sense." Since Wittgenstein rejects the "fruit juicer" method of specifying the content of religious statements, it is impossible to factorize religious beliefs into two kinds of component: the putative "informational" content and the expression of a "doctrine-free" "emotional attitude"[32]. For as we have seen in this essay, such a conception would be at odds with Wittgenstein's entire philosophy of language – it is not just due to the fact that Wittgenstein happens to hold an idiosyncratic view about the nature of religious belief.

Neither does the use of words in a secondary sense have anything to do with the expression of an attitude (as opposed, say, to a "cognitive" belief). If I say that

---

29 Winch has "interpretation," which does not strike me as a good translation of "Auffassung" in this context.

30 See, for example, Nielsen in: Nielsen/Phillips, *Wittgensteinian Fideism?*, 116.

31 See, for example, Cupitt, Don, *The Sea of Faith*, London: SCM Press, 2003.

32 For more on this, see Schönbaumsfeld, Genia, "Wittgenstein and the 'Factorization Model' of Religious Belief," *European Journal for the Philosophy of Religion* 6, no. 1 (2014), 93–110.

the vowel "e" is yellow or that the beginning of Wagner's "Lohengrin overture" is blue, I am not expressing an "attitude" to the letter or the music – I am reporting how things strike me. Similarly, when the religious believer says that "God is omnipresent," he is not expressing an attitude, but reporting his faith. This faith may, of course, engender various attitudes, such as an attitude of submission towards God, but the faith itself is not "just" an attitude, if that means that it is a kind of "content-free" feeling (which is usually what people who make this objection mean).

Consequently, Wittgenstein would happily endorse Kierkegaard's Climacus's remark that:

> I cannot help it that our age has reversed the relation and changed Christianity into a philosophical theory that is to be comprehended and being a Christian into something negligible. To say that Christianity is empty of content because it is not a doctrine is only chicanery. When a believer exists in faith, his existence has enormous content, but not in the sense of a yield in paragraphs'.[33]

Here Climacus is not opposing "doctrine" to "belief," but to "philosophical theory" – i.e., to a set of speculative claims about the behaviour of metaphysical entities. In other words, while Christianity is not a doctrine in this latter sense, this does not imply that it is, therefore, "empty of content." But neither is it possible to specify what Christianity's content consists in independently of making reference to the Christian form of life, in which this "doctrine" is at work. To think otherwise, is just to return to the "fruit juicer" method.

So, contrary to what many commentators think[34], religious concepts and expressions are not, for Wittgenstein, the cognitively empty means to some practical end (say, leading a certain kind of life). Rather, the words and concepts used are as important as anything else. Wittgenstein's point is only that we cannot reach a mature understanding of what these concepts involve independently of looking at the role they play in a religious believer's life. For this role will provide us with the clues to uncover the depth grammar of religious concepts. If we ignore this grammar, on the other hand, we will remain stuck at the level of surface grammar and never get beyond thinking that religion is a hodgepodge of absurd meta-

---

33 Kierkegaard, Søren, *Concluding Unscientific Postscript*, ed. and trans. Howard and Edna Hong, Princeton: Princeton University Press, 1992, 380.
34 See, e.g. Clack, Brian, *An Introduction to Wittgenstein's Philosophy of Religion*, Edinburgh: Edinburgh University Press, 1999; Hyman, *The Gospel According to Wittgenstein*; Gordon, Graham, *Wittgenstein and Natural Religion*, Oxford: Oxford University Press, 2014; McCutcheon, Felicity, *Religion Within the Limits of Language Alone: Wittgenstein on Philosophy and Religion*, London: Ashgate, 2001; Schröder, Severin, "The Tightrope Walker," *Ratio* 20, no. 4 (2007), 442–464.

physical ideas; just as we may never get at the equation of a new curve, if we believe that it consists merely of familiar elements put together in an incoherent way.[35]

Bibliography

Barth, Karl, *Church Dogmatics*, vol. 1, *The Doctrine of the Word of God*, ed. G. W. Bromiley/ T. F. Torrance, London/New York: T&T Clark, 2003.

Clack, Brian, *An Introduction to Wittgenstein's Philosophy of Religion*, Edinburgh: Edinburgh University Press, 1999.

Cottingham, John, "Wittgenstein, Religion and Analytic Philosophy," in: Hans-Johann Glock/John Hyman (eds.), *Wittgenstein and Analytic Philosophy*, 203–227, Oxford: Oxford University Press, 2009.

Cupitt, Don, *The Sea of Faith*, London: SCM Press, 2003.

Diamond, Cora, "Wittgenstein on Religious Belief: The Gulfs Between Us," in: D. Z. Phillips/Mario von der Ruhr (eds.), *Religion and Wittgenstein's Legacy*, 99–138, Aldershot: Ashgate, 2005.

Graham, Gordon, *Wittgenstein and Natural Religion*, Oxford: Oxford University Press, 2014.

Glock, Hans-Johann, *A Wittgenstein Dictionary*, Oxford: Blackwell, 1995.

Hyman, John, "The Gospel According to Wittgenstein," in: Mark Addis/Robert Arrington (eds.), *Wittgenstein and Philosophy of Religion*, 1–11, London: Routledge, 2001.

Kierkegaard, Søren, *Concluding Unscientific Postscript*, ed. and trans. Howard and Edna Hong, Princeton: Princeton University Press, 1992.

Kierkegaard, Søren, *The Point of View*, ed. and trans. Howard and Edna Hong, Princeton: Princeton University Press, 1998.

McCutcheon, Felicity, *Religion Within the Limits of Language Alone: Wittgenstein on Philosophy and Religion*, Aldershot: Ashgate, 2001.

Molnar, Paul, "Barth on the Trinity," in: George Hunsinger/Keith Johnson (eds.), *The Wiley Blackwell Companion to Karl Barth: Barth and Dogmatics Volume 1*, 2–33, Oxford: Wiley Blackwell, 2020.

Phillips, Dewi Zephaniah, *The Concept of Prayer*, London: Routledge, 2015.

Nielsen, Kai/Phillips, Dewi Zephaniah, *Wittgensteinian Fideism?*, London: SCM Press, 2005.

Ridley, Aaron, *The Philosophy of Music: Theme and Variation*, Edinburgh: Edinburgh University Press, 2004.

Rhees, Rush, "On Religion: Notes on Four Conversations With Wittgenstein," *Faith and Philosophy: Journal of the Society of Christian Philosophers* 18, no. 4 (2001), 409–415.

Schönbaumsfeld, Genia, *A Confusion of the Spheres. Kierkegaard and Wittgenstein on Philosophy and Religion*, Oxford: Oxford University Press, 2007.

Schönbaumsfeld, Genia, "Ludwig Wittgenstein," in: Graham Oppy/Nick Trakakis (eds.), *History of Western Philosophy of Religion*, 61–74, Durham: Acumen, 2009.

Schönbaumsfeld, Genia, "Wittgenstein and the 'Factorization Model' of Religious Belief," *European Journal for the Philosophy of Religion* 6, no. 1 (2014), 93–110.

---

35 I would like to thank Mira Sievers, Farid Suleiman and Daniel Weiss for helpful comments on an earlier version of this essay.

Schönbaumsfeld, Genia, "'Meaning-Dawning' in Wittgenstein's Notebooks: A Kierkegaardian Reading and Critique," *British Journal for the History of Philosophy* 26, no. 3 (2018), 540–556.

Schönbaumsfeld, Genia, *Wittgenstein on Religious Belief*, Cambridge: Cambridge University Press, 2023.

Schönbaumsfeld, Genia, "No Gaseous Vertebrates: Wittgenstein's Third Way," in: Duncan Pritchard/ Nuno Venturinha (eds.), *Wittgenstein and the Epistemology of Religion*, Oxford: Oxford University Press, forthcoming.

Schröder, Severin, "The Tightrope Walker," *Ratio* 20, no. 4 (2007), 442–464.

Swinburne, Richard, "Philosophical Theism," in: D. Z. Phillips/Timothy Tessin (eds.), *Philosophy of Religion in the 21st Century*, 1–20, New York: Palgrave, 2001.

Swinburne, Richard, *The Coherence of Theism*, Oxford: Oxford University Press, [2]2016.

Wittgenstein, Ludwig, *Tractatus Logico-Philosophicus*, trans. C.K. Ogden, London: Routledge/Kegan Paul, 1922.

Wittgenstein, Ludwig, *Lectures and Conversations on Aesthetics, Psychology and Religious Belief*, ed. Cyril Barrett, Oxford: Blackwell, 1966.

Wittgenstein, Ludwig, *Culture and Value*, ed. G. H. von Wright, trans. Peter Winch, Oxford: Blackwell, 1977.

Wittgenstein, Ludwig, *Culture and Value, revised edition*, ed. G. H. von Wright, trans. Peter Winch, Oxford: Blackwell, 1998.

Wittgenstein, Ludwig, *Philosophical Investigations*, trans. G.E.M. Anscombe/Peter Hacker/Joachim Schulte, ed. Peter Hacker/Joachim Schulte, Oxford: Blackwell, [4]2009.

Wittgenstein, Ludwig, *Lectures. Cambridge 1930–33*, ed. David Stern/Brian Rogers/Gabriel Citron, New York: Cambridge University Press, 2016.

Suggestions for Further Reading

Cottingham, John, "Wittgenstein, Religion and Analytic Philosophy," in: Hans-Johann Glock/John Hyman (eds.), *Wittgenstein and Analytic Philosophy*, 203–227, Oxford: Oxford University Press, 2009.

Diamond, Cora, "Wittgenstein on Religious Belief: The Gulfs Between Us," in: D. Z. Phillips/Mario von der Ruhr (eds.), *Religion and Wittgenstein's Legacy*, 99–138, Aldershot: Ashgate, 2005.

Hyman, John, "The Gospel According to Wittgenstein," in: Mark Addis/Robert Arrington (eds.), *Wittgenstein and Philosophy of Religion*, 1–11, London: Routledge, 2001.

Nielsen, Kai/Phillips, Dewi Zephaniah, *Wittgensteinian Fideism?*, London: SCM Press, 2005.

Schönbaumsfeld, Genia, *A Confusion of the Spheres. Kierkegaard and Wittgenstein on Philosophy and Religion*, Oxford: Oxford University Press, 2007.

Schönbaumsfeld, Genia, *Wittgenstein on Religious Belief*, Cambridge: Cambridge University Press, 2023.

Daniel H. Weiss

Wittgenstein and the Rabbinic Grammar of God's Name

1 Introduction

In this essay, we will examine the "grammar of God's name" in the context of rabbinic Judaism. When we look at the treatment of God's name in classical rabbinic
literature, we see a pattern in which (drawing upon biblical descriptions) God has
a specific proper name, and yet human beings (currently) are not in a position to
utter that name. So, while there is no uttering God's proper name, various practices are retained (in both writing and speech) that emphasize that God does have
a name.

   In the first three sections of this essay, we will draw out various theological
and grammatical dynamics of this understanding and use of God's name, without
yet commenting on the ways in which these dynamics could appear conceptually
controversial from a certain point of view. Following this, however, we will look
at reasons why some might view (and have viewed) the idea of God having a
name as an inherently problematic notion. Specifically, there exists a longstand-
ing stream of philosophical and theological tradition in which the idea of God as
"most high" and as "the creator of all, and not a created being" goes along with
God being nameless or "beyond names." In such a framework, the idea of a god
who has a name would necessarily imply that such a god cannot be the creator of
all. A god that has a name is not an inherent problem if you don't also claim that
god to be creator – but it is a problem if you want to claim that a named god is
also the creator. Hence, there is a philosophical-theological tendency (which can
be discerned in certain Christian and Jewish traditions) to say that God must be
beyond names. In other words, it seems that it is necessary for God not to have a
name in order to preserve certain "desirable" things that you want to maintain
about God.

   From this perspective, the rabbinic (and biblical) presentation can seem "confused" or "still stuck in an older or primitive conception" or "not yet arrived at a
full understanding." It may be reaching toward the "higher" notion of God's transcendence, but has not yet fully left behind the "lower" understanding, as evi-
denced by its retention of the idea of God having a name. This perspective is not
able to view the rabbinic preservation of both elements together as a knowing
and sophisticated position, and might instead say: "What would be the point of preserving the idea of God's name? If they elsewhere do assert their recognition of

https://doi.org/10.1515/9783111501611-003

God's transcendent status as creator, why do they not simply embrace namelessness fully?"

However, drawing both upon Wittgenstein's notions of grammar and grammatical illusions and upon modern Jewish religious-philosophical thought, we will see that the rabbinic pattern can be cast not as a "limited understanding" or "backwards conception," but as linked to a robust but *different* conception. By contrast, the attitude that insists that the creator God *cannot* have a name may be shaped by "illusions" similar to those Wittgenstein diagnoses in certain modes of "doing philosophy." In particular, we will draw upon Wittgenstein's criticism of the tendency to think that if a concept retains unclear aspects when one reflects on it theoretically, there must be something problematic about the concept itself. Against this, Wittgenstein affirms that various concepts can rightly be treated as fully legitimate and valuable even if one is unable to arrive at a fully clear and consistent theoretical account of them, and that one ought not to treat these types of clarity and consistency as a universally required criterion for our concepts. In light of this, the rabbinic pattern and practice can instead serve to illuminate rich theological understandings of prayer and interpersonal relation to God that would not be discernible if one insists on forcing the data into certain preconceived metaphysical frameworks.

2 Biblical Dynamics of God's Name

Before we examine a range of classical rabbinic statements and practices that relate to God's name, it is worthwhile to contextualize these discussions by first clarifying some biblical precedents. Throughout the Hebrew Bible, the God who created the world and is described as relating to Adam, Noah, Abraham, Moses, David, etc., is repeatedly referred to via the word "YHVH." Furthermore, in multiple places, this term "YHVH" is explicitly asserted to be God's "name." For example, in Ex. 3:13, Moses encounters God in the burning bush, and says to God, "When I come to the Israelites and say to them, 'The God of your fathers has sent me to you,' and they ask me, 'What is His name [*mah shemo*]?' what shall I say to them?" In Ex. 3:15, God tells Moses: "Thus shall you speak to the Israelites: YHVH, the God of your fathers, the God of Abraham, the God of Isaac, and the God of Jacob, has sent me to you: This is My name forever [*zeh shemi le'olam*], this is My appellation for all eternity." Likewise, in Ex. 6:2–3, God says to Moses, "I am YHVH: I appeared to Abraham, Isaac, and Jacob as El Shaddai, but I did not make my name YHVH [*shemi YHVH*] known to them." In God's subsequent self-presentation in the Ten Commandments, God says, "I, YHVH, am your God, who took you out of the land of Egypt." (Ex. 20:2).

And, to take one more example, in Is. 42:8, God announces, "I am YHVH, that is My name [*hu shemi*]; and My glory I will not give to another, nor My praise to graven images."

Elsewhere in the biblical text, there appears to be encouragement to engage with God in relation to his specific name, e.g., Ps. 30:4, "Sing praises to YHVH, O you his faithful ones, and give thanks to his holy name;" or Ps. 34:3, "O magnify YHVH with me, and let us exalt his name together." Thus, from a straightforward reading of the biblical text, it would appear that the God who created the world has a specific name, and that the Israelites address God in prayer and worship through this specific name.

Furthermore, across the various texts of the Hebrew Bible there does not seem to be any attempt to claim that God is "nameless" or "has no name" or "is beyond names." However, there are various places that point to indications that there can be proper or improper ways of using God's name. Thus, Ex. 20:7 (and Deut. 5:11) states, "You shall not make wrongful use of the name of YHVH your God, for YHVH will not acquit anyone who misuses his name." Lev. 22:32 states, "You shall not profane my holy name, that I may be sanctified among the people of Israel: I, YHVH, am the one who sanctifies you." In addition to avoiding improper use of God's name, the Israelites are also told to avoid calling upon the names of any other god: "Be attentive to all that I have said to you. Do not invoke the name of other gods; do not let it be heard on your lips" (Ex. 23:13).

Finally, one additional theme in the Hebrew Bible in relation to God's name is the idea that God's name is associated particularly with a specific location, namely, the Temple in Jerusalem. Thus, 1 Kings 9:3 recounts God's statement to Solomon, after Solomon finishes building the Temple: "YHVH said to him, 'I have heard your prayer and your plea, which you made before me; I have consecrated this house that you have built, and put my name there forever; my eyes and my heart will be there for all time.'" This location-specific element will be significant when considering the rabbinic treatment of God's name.

3 Dynamics of God's Name in Classical Rabbinic Literature

The texts of classical rabbinic literature (edited between the third and sixth centuries CE) are shaped, on the one hand, by a sustained engagement with the biblical texts, and, on the other hand, by efforts to interpret and apply these biblical texts in their own time and context, a context in which the Temple in Jerusalem was no longer in existence, having been destroyed in the first century CE during the Roman destruction of Jerusalem.

The classical rabbinic texts retain the basic biblical idea that God has a specific name. However, they also attest to a notion, not explicitly thematized in the biblical texts, of a "substitute" term (*kinui*) that is pronounced in various contexts instead of God's actual name. Thus, Mishnah Sotah 7:6 states:

> How is the priestly blessing [pronounced]? In the province [i.e., outside of the Temple] it is said as three blessings, but in the Temple as one blessing. In the Temple the name is uttered as it is written [*kikhtavo*], but in the province in its substituted name [*ve-khinuyo*].

In this presentation, when the priestly blessing (Numbers 6:23–27) was said in the Temple, the three times the term "YHVH" appears in those verses, the name was pronounced "as it is written" in the Torah scroll, in other words, with the consonants Yud-Hey-Vav-Hey. However, outside of the Temple, that same term was pronounced "with its substitute [*kinui*]": it was uttered as *Adonai* (my Lord), rather than "as it is written" in the written Torah scroll.

In this presentation of a distinction between how God's name was uttered "in the Temple" and "outside of the Temple," the Mishnah nonetheless portrays a world in which the uttering of God's specific name is something one might potentially encounter – if one happens to find oneself in the Temple, that is. However, since the rabbinic texts were redacted long after the Temple's destruction, the stipulation that God's specific name is legitimately pronounced only in the Temple entails that, by the time of the Mishnah's redaction, there was *no* existing space in which God's name could be legitimately pronounced "as it is written," and thus in *all* existing spaces, God's name is to be pronounced with its substitute of "*Adonai*/my Lord."

The rabbinic opposition to pronouncing God's actual name is underscored in Mishnah Sanhedrin 10:1, in a discussion of the small number of categories of people who do *not* have a "share in the world to come." Here, Abba Shaul states that "one who pronounces the name with its letters" is included under this sharply negative theological judgment. Here, the negative judgment is applied not to "one who pronounces the name with its letters outside of the Temple," but simply to "one who pronounces the name with its letters," implying a rabbinic understanding that the current state of existence is one in which pronouncing God's name as it is written can *only* be an inappropriate action.

Notably, this practice of non-pronunciation as "YHVH" and substitute pronunciation as *Adonai* nevertheless takes place in a context in which Jews would be *encountering* God's name as "YHVH" on regular basis: namely, when they encounter God's name in the written text of the Torah scroll: even though it is not *pronounced* as it is written, the visual encounter with God's name serves to underscore the idea that God does *have* a specific name. This in turn may generate a certain tension for people between their visual-textual experience and their oral-auditory experience and practice.

Such a tension is thematized by the following commentary found in the Babylonian Talmud (hereafter BT), Pesaḥim 50a:

> [The verse states: "On that day YHVH will be one] and His name one" (Zech. 14:9).] What is the meaning of 'one' here? Does that mean his name is not now one? Rav Naḥman bar Yitz-ḥak said: The world to come is not like this world: in this world, God's name is written with Yud-Hey [i.e., YHVH] but is read [aloud] with Alef-Dalet [i.e., *Adonai*]. But in the world to come, it will all be one: it will be read [aloud] with Yud-Hey and written with Yud-Hey.

Here, the text emphasizes a duality (in the present world) between the way God's name is written in the Torah scroll and the way God's name is read aloud. Thus, currently, God's name is not "one." However, the text also emphasizes that in the messianic-eschatological future, things will be different, and God's name will be read aloud in the same way as it is written. Thus, God's actual name was previously pronounced in the past (in the Temple), and will be pronounced in the future, even though it is not pronounced in the present.

Importantly, the non-pronunciation of God's actual name in the present appears to correspond to the fact that, according to classical rabbinic understandings, God's "direct divine presence" (the *shekhinah*) was removed from the earth following the destruction of the Temple, having previously been locationally centered in the holy of holies in the Temple itself. While God is still "present with Israel" in a weaker sense, as well as "present with" humanity more broadly and with all of creation, the stronger sense of the presence of the *shekhinah* is understood as currently absent (*silluq ha-shekhinah*), and will not return until the messianic future.[1] In the rabbinic portrayal, therefore, the pronunciation of God's name appears to correlate with times and places in which God's presence is directly present in the stronger sense.[2]

---

1 Cf. BT Yoma 39a–b, in which the explicit use of God's name even in the Temple ceased following the death of Simeon the Righteous (ca. 3rd century BCE), a shift that also corresponded to the ceasing of regularly-occurring miracles in the Temple, indicating a lessening of God's direct divine presence.

2 For a recent study of the name of God in rabbinic thought, see Ben-Sasson, Hillel, *Understanding YHWH: The Name of God in Biblical, Rabbinic, and Medieval Jewish Thought*, London: Palgrave Macmillan, 2019.

4 The Grammar of God's Name

Having presented a range of data from rabbinic texts, we can now comment on initial aspects of the "grammar" of God's name.[3] One pronounces God's actual name in certain physical locations, but in other locations, one uses the substitute *Adonai*. Likewise, one pronounces God's actual name in certain time periods, but in others one uses *Adonai*. Thus, there is no place-neutral or atemporal use of God's name – it is specifically place- and time-dependent.

We can compare this "grammar" to the everyday grammar that distinguishes between the use of the second-person and the third-person: if I am speaking directly *to* a certain person, I use the second person (you), but if I am speaking *about* that same person to someone else, I use the third person (he or she). Thus, it would be "grammatically wrong," when talking directly to a certain person about that person's height, to say to them, "She are tall;" instead, I would say, "You are tall." Likewise, when talking about that person to someone else, one wouldn't say, "You is tall," but rather "She is tall."

This comparison is also useful for highlighting the correlation of "direct presence" in the use of God's actual name *versus* the use of *Adonai*: just as one typically uses the second-person when a person is present before you, and you are speaking directly to that person, but one uses the third person when that person is not present, so likewise one uses God's actual name in a place and time when God's *shekhinah* is "directly present," and one uses the substitute *Adonai* in a place/time when God's direct presence (in that stronger sense) is not present.[4] In this regard, one could potentially conceive of the typical everyday grammatical practice as: the terms

---

3 Note that the comparisons and analogies in this section are not intended to "make sense of" or resolve the potentially problematic aspects of the rabbinic concept, but simply to illuminate additional aspects of the observed conceptual patterns. Addressing "problematic" aspects will follow in the subsequent sections.

4 As with the potentially problematic aspects of the idea of God having a name, so too the classical rabbinic treatment of God's presence as more directly present in certain times or places than in other times and places could appear to some (including various subsequent Jewish thinkers) as philosophically or conceptually problematic, and as seeming to engage in a problematic type of anthropomorphism. For various relevant treatments of the "problem" of rabbinic anthropomorphism, see, e.g., Lorberbaum, Yair, *In God's Image: Myth, Theology, and Law in Classical Judaism*, Cambridge: Cambridge University Press, 2015, 13–45; Kadushin, Max, *The Rabbinic Mind*, Binghamton: Global Publications, 2001 [1972], 273–287; Rosenzweig, Franz, "A Note on Anthropomorphisms: in Response to the Encyclopedia Judaica's Article" [1928], in his *God, Man and the World: Lectures and Essays*, ed. and trans. Barbara Galli, Syracuse: Syracuse University Press, 1998, 135–145.; Wettstein, Howard, *The Significance of Religious Experience*, New York: Oxford University Press, 2012; Stern, David, "*Imitatio Hominis*: Anthropomorphism and the Character(s) of God in Rabbinic Literature," *Prooftexts* 12, no. 2 (1992), 151–174.

"he" or "she" constitute a "substitute" for times/places when the other person is not present, and therefore one cannot use that person's "actual" pronoun of "you."

One other potential grammatical analogy from everyday language could be the formal *versus* informal/initimate/familiar forms of the second person singular, such as *vous* and *tu* in French or *Sie* and *Du* in German. "Sie" and "Du" are *both* terms that can be used as second-person address, with the difference typically depending on the specific social and personal relation between the speaker and the addressee. In some ways, this could be more analogous to the rabbinic grammar of God's name, insofar as "YHVH" and *Adonai* would *both* be used in second-person address (whereas in the previous analogy, "he/she" versus "you" are not both terms used in direct address). And, the use of "YHVH" in the context of direct divine presence could appear to have some parallels with the "intimate/familiar" use of *Du* or *tu*. However, there can also be disanalogies: the rabbinic presentation is that "YHVH" was previously used, but is not used currently, so that there has been an overall shift away from "YHVH" to *Adonai* (even though, according to the rabbis, *Adonai* would have been used in most contexts even at the time when the Temple was standing). By contrast, with *Du/Sie* or *tu/vous*, a relation would more typically begin with *Sie/vous* and *later* move to *Du/tu*, but a relation would not typically shift from *Du/tu* to *Sie/vous*. However, even though these analogies (second vs third person, or *du* vs *Sie*) are not perfect, they are nevertheless helpful in aiding us to reflect in a "grammatical" mode about the rabbinic presentation of the "proper" use of God's name.

In addition, we can remark on the "strange" practical situation of a "grammatical rule" that is never put into practice in one's own experience. Because the Temple has been destroyed, the rabbinic texts are situated in a time and context in which there is *no* appropriate situation in which a person might speak or hear God's actual name. Instead, in this context, in situations of addressing God in prayer or reading God's name from the Torah scroll, one will *always* speak or hear it spoken as *Adonai* and *never* speak it or hear it spoken "as it is written." A context in which one *sometimes* hears one name used for God and *sometimes* hears a substitute is thus significantly different, in experiential terms, from a context in which one *never* hears God's "actual" name and *always* hears a substitute – even if one also 'knows' that in principle or in theory God has an actual name that is different from what one has always heard. Would this be analogous to the idea that there is in theory a "fourth person" form of speaking, but that in practice one only encounters situations in which the first, second or third person forms are appropriate? Or to the idea that there is an additional form of "you-address" beyond *Sie* and *Du*, but that no one today ever finds themselves in a situation in which it would be appropriate to use it?

To be sure, the idea of "a 'grammatical form' that people know about but simply never encounter an appropriate situation to use" may in some ways sound "empty," perhaps akin to the notion of a "private language" critiqued by Wittgenstein. Yet, one key difference is the rabbinic presentation incorporates the past and the future into its account: people today and in the rabbis' own context may live their whole lives hearing only *Adonai* and never hear God's name "as it is written" – yet hearing or speaking God's name is *not* treated as something "impossible" or something that "humans cannot appropriately do." Rather, it is presented as: this *did* happen in the past, and *will* happen again in the messianic future, even though it is not *presently* possible to encounter a situation in which it can be appropriately used. So "knowing about" God's name does also correlate to a "practice that *can actually be* experienced," even if it does not *happen to be* experienced in the present era. And, in this regard, the repeated experiential practice of visually encountering God's name written as Y-H-V-H in the Torah scroll serves a continual reminder of God's actual name that can be spoken, has been spoken, and will be spoken, even though it currently is not spoken.

5 God's Name as a Problem

Having framed some of the basic "grammar" of the rabbinic presentation of the practice of using God's name, we can now consider some deeper theological implications that we can understand as embedded in this "grammatical" pattern. However, before doing so, we should first consider a major theological objection that can be raised against the rabbinic approach as a whole. As we have seen, the biblical text presents the God who created the world and everything in it as having a specific name, spelled Y-H-V-H. The classical rabbinic texts follow this basic idea of God having a specific name, while simply adding more detailed stipulations about when and in what contexts that name can appropriately be spoken, and in what contexts the substitute of *Adonai* ought to be used instead. However, the rabbinic texts themselves were compiled in a time period where the notion of "God most high, the God of all creation" having a specific name would have been viewed by many people as an absurd and self-contradictory idea. As Kendall Soulen has highlighted, a view that had become increasingly widespread in pagan thought and philosophy was the belief "that the deity could in principle have no name (. . .) God was, in the language of middle Platonism, strictly 'unnamable and ineffable' (*akatonomaston te kai arrēton*)."[5]

---

5 Soulen, Kendall, *The Divine Name(s) and the Holy Trinity: Distinguishing the Voices*, Louisville: Westminster John Knox Press, 2011, 49.

While the texts of the New Testament generally seem to have preserved the biblical idea of God having a specific name,[6] many Christian authors after the time of the New Testament texts aligned themselves instead with the notion of God as "nameless" or "beyond names and naming."[7] Thus, to take the example of Justin Martyr, the prominent second-century Christian writer, we find strong assertions such as, "For no one can utter the name of the ineffable God; and if any one dare to say that there is a name, he raves with a hopeless madness."[8] Justin likewise writes:

> But we have received by tradition that God does not need the material offerings which men can give, seeing, indeed, that He Himself is the provider of all things. And we have been taught, and are convinced, and do believe, that He accepts those only who imitate the excellences which reside in Him, temperance, and justice, and philanthropy, and as many virtues as are peculiar to a God who is called by no proper name.[9]

Similarly, he asserts:

> But to the Father of all, who is unbegotten there is no name given. For by whatever name He be called, He has as His elder the person who gives Him the name. But these words Father, and God, and Creator, and Lord, and Master, are not names, but appellations derived from His good deeds and functions.[10]

---

6 Soulen, *Divine Name(s)*, 13, 31, 33–34. See also Soulen, "Jesus and the Divine Name," *Union Seminary Quarterly Review* 65, no. 1–2 (2015), 47–58; Soulen, "'Go Tell Pharaoh,' or Why Empires Prefer a Nameless God," in: Jürgen Moltmann/Timothy Eberhart/Matthew W. Charlton (eds.), *The Economy of Salvation: Essays in Honour of M. Douglas Meeks*, 58–70, Eugene: Cascade, 2015; Soulen, *Irrevocable: The Name of God and the Unity of the Christian Bible*, Minneapolis: Fortress Press, 2022.

7 Soulen, *Divine Name(s)*, 49–53.

8 Justin Martyr, *First Apology*, 61. This and subsequent passages from Justin Martyr drawn from: Alexander Roberts/James Donaldson/A. Cleveland Coxe (eds.), *Ante-Nicene Fathers*, vol. 1, Buffalo: Christian Literature Publishing Co., 1885.

9 Justin Martyr, *First Apology*, 10.

10 Justin Martyr, *Second Apology*, 6. See also Justin Martyr, *Horatory Address to the Greeks*, 21. Note that when Justin is engaging the biblical text, the Greek versions of the Hebrew Bible that he engages were likely ones that rendered God's name as *kyrios* (Lord). By contrast, as Soulen notes, various Jewish translations of the Hebrew Bible into Greek preserved God's name in Hebrew or Aramaic characters (as the Tetragrammaton, YHVH) without writing an orthographic substitute, even though such Greek-speaking communities would have substituted *kyrios* when reading the text aloud (*Divine Name(s)*, 30–34). This may have been the case with the Greek version of the Hebrew Bible/Old Testament used by many of the New Testament authors. In such versions of the Greek text (as in the rabbinic versions of the Torah scroll), it would be harder to ignore the fact that, orthographically speaking, God does indeed appear to have a proper name. By contrast, in the version used by Justin and subsequent Christian writers, God's name is written simply as *kyrios* (Κύριος; or sometimes written via a special abbreviation $\overline{ΚΣ}$). Thus, in the written version of Justin's text, with no indication of the Tetragrammaton, God's name could eas-

Justin's basic reasoning, which is in line with broader Platonic trends, is that God can have no name (other than names that humans apply to God by convention) because God is "the Father of all," i.e., the creator of everything – but God is himself uncreated and unbegotten. Names are "given" by a older or superior person to a younger or dependent person – so to assert that God has a name is equivalent to treating God as a created being, who was given a name by "someone prior to God," which is an absurd notion. In this framework, God is the creator and provider of all things, but is not in need of being "provided with" anything by any other, and hence cannot have a name, which is inherently something that someone is "provided with" by another.

Importantly, in the pagan Greco-Roman philosophically-influenced context, the notion of a higher "nameless God" stood specifically in contrast to the named gods of Greek and Roman mythology. Thus, a "named god" would have been viewed as corresponding to the "less philosophically advanced" mindset of the *hoi polloi* – whereas those who are "educated" would "realize" that the "true" understanding of God, going beyond the stories of mythology with their named characters, is that God is in fact uncreated and is therefore nameless. One may encounter the cultural phenomenon of named gods, but it points to a limited understanding that has not yet progressed to the true comprehension of God's namelessness. Thus, a god with a name, by necessity, cannot be the true creator of all, and the true creator of all, by necessity, cannot have a name. Put differently, if you want to uphold God's status as creator and not as created, you *must* robustly reject any notion of God having a name.

With this cultural backdrop in mind, the way of describing God in the biblical text can come to appear, from this perspective, as very problematic. We have seen that throughout the Hebrew Bible, God seems to be unabashedly presented as having a specific name, YHVH. Thus, someone reading these texts might say: "The people who have composed these texts seem to think that God has a name! But this shows that in fact they aren't relating themselves to the true creator God, but to a primitive notion of the deity." Even if one were to point out that various texts in the Hebrew Bible do present God as the "creator of all," the interlocutor could respond, "Yes, but this indicates only that these texts have *begun* to work toward the idea that there would be one creator of all – but at the same time they

---

ily come across simply as an "appellation" of "Lord," with no indication that God has a distinct proper name. Thus, the orthographic practice of both writing and pronouncing God's name via *kyrios* could have more readily lent itself to the conceptual notion that God has no proper name (but only appellations), while the orthographic practice of writing God's name with the Tetragrammaton but pronouncing it as *kyrios* or *Adonai* may have contributed to preserving the conceptual notion that God does have a proper name.

still remain largely entangled in the notion of a named (and therefore 'lower') god. If they had truly arrived at a clear understanding of the creator of all, they would also have realized that this entails God's namelessness." Thus, the Hebrew Bible could appear to stand closer to the level of Greek and Roman mythology, with their "named gods," and to fall short of the "true" understanding of God as creator of all.

Now, even starting with the inheritance of the biblical text – as Justin Martyr, for instance, also does – it would be possible to try to "interpret away" the apparent "named" status of God in the Bible, and to assert that, despite outward appearances, the biblical text, when properly understood, doesn't actually hold to the (uneducated and unsophisticated) idea of God as having a name. Many Christian writers in late antiquity did indeed take this un-naming approach, a process which they viewed as necessary if they wanted to uphold the God of the Bible as the true God of creation and not as a mere created being.

Yet, the classical rabbinic texts do not appear to have taken this path. If anything, they could seem to have taken a step backwards! By detailing and distinguishing between appropriate and inappropriate uses of God's name, it further reinforces the idea that God indeed has a special name: the care and concern that is enjoined in relation to the use of God's name serves to underscore that this *really is* God's name, and not merely a human convention. Although the rabbinic texts do also repeatedly emphasize God's supreme nature as the one who alone created the world, their continued and even expanded engagement with the idea of God having a name could seemingly cast them as still trapped in a backward and unenlightened understanding of God.[11] At a minimum, it would seem strange that they would continue to treat God as having a name *while also* affirming God's "transcendent" status as creator of all: "Could they not see that these two notions were in contradiction to one another, and that to properly uphold the latter one must, by logical necessity, reject the former? Perhaps, sadly, they had sim-

---

11 As Soulen notes, the practice of the non-pronunciation of God's proper name, in addition to being prominent in New Testament texts, has continued in various forms in Christian tradition up to the present day, including, e.g., in a 2008 statement from the Vatican, prohibiting the pronunciation of the Tetragrammaton in Roman Catholic worship contexts (Soulen, *Irrevocable*, 110). At the same time, various other voices in Christian contexts today have inclined more toward the "nameless God" orientation, in which the notion of God having a proper name is often cast as a backwards or archaic position that ought to be overcome (Soulen, *Irrevocable*, 165). Thus, in addition to shedding light on rabbinic Jewish theological traditions, our analysis here may also be relevant for illuminating dynamics of Christian theological tradition as well. In addition, although less directly connected to the Tetragrammaton, the present analysis may also be relevant to Islamic traditions of naming God and the idea of "God's greatest name."

ply not yet freed themselves from the earlier inherited understanding and were not aware of its problematic nature."[12]

6 Modern Jewish Philosophical Theology

If a person is convinced that retaining the idea of God having a specific name is a retrograde vestige that ought properly to be overcome as one gains in philosophical sophistication, the apparent "failure" of the classical rabbinic texts to do so could potentially be attributed to the fact that they are written in an idiom that differs from typical "philosophical" writing, and that they do not explicitly cite and engage with classical Greek philosophical texts (e.g., Platonic, Aristotelian, Stoic traditions). If they had explicitly engaged with the latter traditions, one might think, they would surely have recognized the error of their ways and would have affirmed the namelessness of the transcendent God.

Yet, this assumption is called sharply into question when we look at a range of modern Jewish thinkers who engaged closely with such philosophical traditions, and yet continued to affirm the idea of God's name. To take one example, Abraham Joshua Heschel, the prominent twentieth-century thinker, who received his PhD in philosophy from the University of Berlin and whose writings are shaped by close engagement with philosophical thought (particularly traditions of phenomenology), adamantly affirmed not only the appropriateness, but also the importance of the tradition of God's name:

> The God of Israel is a name, not a notion. There is a difference between a "name" and a "notion." I am suggesting to you: don't teach notions of God, teach the name of God. A notion applies to all objects of similar properties. A name applies to an individual. The name "God

---

12 Against this portrayal of classical rabbinic texts continuing to affirm the idea of God's name out of ignorance or naïveté, various scholars have emphasized that rabbinic texts display awareness that various of their theological orientations could be viewed as problematic by others. Thus, it is more appropriate to view the rabbinic stance as constituting an aware and reflective position rather than assuming it to be a naïve one. See, e.g., Hayes, Christine, "Displaced Self-Perceptions: The Deployment of Minim and Romans in b. Sanhedrin 90b–91a," in: Hayim Lapin (ed.), *Religious and Ethnic Communities in Later Roman Palestine*, 249–289, Bethesda: University Press of Maryland, 1998, 286: "The rabbis exhibit a high level of exegetical self-consciousness, an ability to see themselves and their exegetical activities as they may have been seen by outsiders"; Labendz, Jenny, *Socratic Torah: Non-Jews in Rabbinic Intellectual Culture*, Oxford: Oxford University Press, 2013, 209: "[I]t is clear that some rabbis in both Palestine and Babylonia, at least at times, show a sensitivity to the individual personalities, backgrounds, and epistemological assumptions of the various people to whom they communicate knowledge."

of Israel" applies to the one and only God of all men. A notion describes, defines; a name evokes. A notion is derived from a generalization; a name is learned through acquaintance. A notion you can conceive; a name you call (. . .). [N]otions and the name of God of Israel are profoundly incompatible. All notions crumble when applied to Him.[13]

Here, rather than seeking to avoid the fact that rabbinic tradition treats God as having a name, Heschel takes the bull by the horns and insists that "name" is highly appropriate in connection with the Jewish way of relating to God. While Justin Martyr was concerned that having a name would lower God to the level of created beings, Heschel emphasizes that God having a specific name grounds the Jewish practice of calling upon God in prayer in the framework of a personal and interpersonal relationship. It orients relation to God as relation to a unique individual rather than as relation to an abstract or general concept. The act of addressing a God who has a name (even if one uses a substitute like *Adonai*) performatively puts one into dialogical relation to God: the act of named address is structurally bound up with the possibility that the addressee is able to listen to what you say. Likewise, the type of trust or confidence that one has in a named individual differs from the way in which one relates to a notion.[14] Relating to God in terms of a name reinforces the sense that asking God for mercy or compassion is something that makes sense, whereas to attribute mercy or compassion to a general or abstract notion would be a category error.

In a related context, Heschel comments on the Talmudic dictum "When you pray, know before whom you stand [*lifnei mi atem omdim*]" (BT Berachot 28b). Noting that the statement says "before whom" (*lifnei mi*) rather than "before

---

13 Heschel, Abraham Joshua, "Jewish Theology," in: Susannah Heschel (ed.), *Moral Grandeur and Spiritual Audacity*, New York: Farrar, Straus, and Giroux, 1996, 162. See also Heschel, "The God of Israel and Christian Renewal," in: *Moral Grandeur and Spiritual Audacity*, 268, and cf. Heschel, "The God Israel and Christian Renewal, 269: "You can think of Him only by seeking to be present to Him. You cannot define him, you can only invoke Him. He is not a notion but a name." See also Heschel, *God in Search of Man: A Philosophy of Judaism*, New York: Farrar, Straus, and Giroux, 1976, 64, on God's name and the restrictions on its pronunciation.
14 In relation to Heschel's affirmation of God's name as reinforcing the idea of relation to God as relation to a unique individual, some could potentially respond: "Yes, 'name' does indeed go along with 'individual' – but both 'name' and 'individual' are similarly problematic in relation to the God who is qualitatively different from all created beings!" Thus, in affirming both of these concepts in relation to God, Heschel is knowingly resisting the assumption that these *must* be treated as incompatible with the idea of God as creator of all. As we will see below, Heschel, as well as Hermann Cohen, recognize that linking these concepts to God can indeed create a type of tension with the idea of God's difference from created beings – however, they do not treat this tension as inherently problematic or fatal, or as something to be overcome; rather, it can function as a fruitful and productive tension.

what" (*lifnei mah*), Heschel asserts, "To have said before *what* would have contradicted the spirit of Jewish prayer (. . .). If God is a *what*, a power, the sum total of values, how could we pray to it? An 'I' does not pray to an 'it.'"[15] Here, Heschel emphasizes that God is not a "what" or an "it," but rather a "whom" and a "you." The act of praying-to makes sense only in the framework of a relation of an "I" to a "you." This interpersonal framing, of relating to God as a "you" rather than an "it," appears to parallel Heschel's insistence that one ought to teach about the God of Israel as a name rather than a notion. For Heschel, upholding the idea of God's name helps to preserve and underscore the importance of relating to and addressing God personally, as a unique "you" that the human individual (qua "I") can call upon in contexts of gratitude, concern, frustration, confusion, and hope. Conversely, abandoning the idea of God as having a name would undermine the act of relating to and calling upon God in a personal framing as a "you."

In defending the idea of God's name, Heschel is aware this idea would be viewed as problematic by certain types of philosophical thought-traditions. He writes, "'The God of Israel' is a *name*, not a notion, and the difference between the two is perhaps the difference between Jerusalem and Athens."[16] Drawing on the tropes of "Athens" and "Jerusalem," Heschel acknowledges that in one thought tradition, it would be inappropriate to understand God as having a name, while nevertheless insisting that in the other thought tradition, it would be inappropriate *not* to understand God as having a name. While both of these "traditions" have shaped Jewish theological reflection over the centuries, and while Heschel himself engages with both of them,[17] his framing seeks to relativize the assumption that "name" cannot appropriately apply to God as creator of all the world. Challenging the idea that "name" and "the creator of all the world" are incompatible simply as a matter of inescapable logical necessity, he recasts this supposed incompatibility not as universally or inherently the case, but as characteristic of one particular conceptual framework – while also affirming the validity of an alternative conceptual framework in which one can and should affirm God as creator of all the world *and* as having a name. The fact that Heschel takes this stance while also seeking to engage

---

15 Heschel, "The Spirit of Jewish Prayer," in: *Moral Grandeur*, 109, italics in the original.
16 Heschel, "The God of Israel and Christian Renewal," 268.
17 Heschel does not treat "philosophy" as linked with Athens rather than with Jerusalem; indeed, he incorporates this term prominently into the titles of two of his most well-known books (*Man is not Alone: A Philosophy of Religion* and *God in Search of Man: A Philosophy of Judaism*). Instead, he seems to treat "Athens" as linked with a *certain type of* philosophy, such that there can be another type of philosophizing that is more linked to what Heschel calls "Jerusalem," and which does not insist on rejecting notions such as God having a name, simply because they appear "logically inconsistent." As we shall see, this latter type of philosophy might be more akin to the type that Wittgenstein seeks to affirm in his "grammatical" approach to "doing philosophy."

philosophically shows that "God having a name" is not simply a position held by people unfamiliar with philosophical reflection, or by people who treat dismiss the importance of philosophical concerns. Rather, Heschel is aware of philosophical concerns about anthropomorphism and seeks to differentiate biblical and rabbinic thought from anthropomorphism[18] – and yet he nevertheless asserts the legitimacy and importance of God's name.

From the perspective of Heschel's construal, then, the fact that classical rabbinic literature continues to treat God as having a name does not mark a "primitive vestige" that ought properly to be overcome via a greater level of sophistication, education, or intellectual capability. Rather, the rabbinic emphasis on God as having a name can be understood as part and parcel of adamantly holding fast to the practice of relating to God personally in prayer, of addressing God as a "you" to whom one can pour forth one's hopes and prayers, with the confidence that such address will not go unheard. If read with the assumption that God having a name is incompatible with God being the creator of all, then the rabbinic texts will necessarily appear mired in backwardness. By contrast, if read without this assumption, one can recognize their treatment of God's name as instead indicative of the texts' promotion of intimate, personal relation to God.[19]

However, while Heschel's approach would seem to have much to recommend it in terms of its fostering of prayer and religious vibrancy within a communal

---

18 See, for instance, Heschel's assertions in relation to biblical prophetic language in *The Prophets*, New York: Perennial, 2001: "God's unconditional concern for justice is not an anthropomorphism. Rather, man's concern for justice is a theomorphism" (349); "To speak about God as if he were a person does not necessarily mean to personify Him, to stamp Him in the image of a person" (350); "The statements about pathos are not a compromise – ways of accommodating higher meanings to the lower level of human understanding. They are rather the accommodation of words to higher meanings" (348); "This was due to the complex nature of prophetic language, which of necessity combines otherness and likeness, uniqueness and comparability, in speaking about God" (347). In contexts in which there is an "unawareness of the transcendence and uniqueness of God," (346) the prophetic way of speaking could be dangerous. However, within the prophetic framework, "Since the human could never be regarded as divine, there was no danger that the language of pathos would distort the difference between God and man (346)" Thus, "We are inclined to question the legitimacy of applying the term anthropopathy to the prophetic statements about the divine pathos" (346).
19 The promotion of personal relation to God need not be the only role played by the rabbinic emphasis on God having a name; this emphasis could also play additional roles within the rabbinic conceptual framework. In addition, while it is difficult to prove conclusively from the classical rabbinic texts themselves, it is certainly plausible that the classical rabbis were aware that other thinkers in their time period insisted that the creator of all *cannot* have a name – and that their bold affirmation of God's having a name, without treating this a "problem," may instead reflect a willingness, like Heschel's, consciously and actively to resist this insistence.

context, one could potentially object that his stance simply dodges the issue. Such objections might run something like: "It is all well and good that the idea of God having a name goes along with relating to God personally and as a 'you' – but this does not resolve the concern that treating God as having a name still structurally casts God as a created being rather than as the creator. A personal relation with the being you worship, whatever its seeming advantages, is not worth it if it means that you have aligned yourself not with the transcendent creator of all but with some non-transcendent being. Even if you *claim* to be treating God as the creator of all, conceiving of God as having a name functionally undermines this claim and results in a confused and incoherent understanding of God." Thus, while Heschel can maintain that "God as a name rather than a notion" represents an alternative conceptual framework, the question still remains as to whether such a conceptual framework is fatally marked by a problematic inconsistency and incoherence. Could it be, therefore, that one ultimately needs to choose between the idea of God as having a name and the idea of God as creator?

In attempting to address this concern raised by Heschel's approach, we can be aided by the reflections of an earlier twentieth-century Jewish thinker, Hermann Cohen. In his *Religion of Reason out of the Sources of Judaism*, Cohen asserts, in language very similar to Heschel's, that the difference between the approach to God in "Jewish religion" (which he links especially to biblical and classical rabbinic texts) and in "Greek speculation" (i.e., the texts of classical Greek philosophical tradition) is "the transformation of the neuter into a person," a difference that he likewise formulates as "the transformation of an abstraction into a person."[20] As in Heschel's reference to "Jerusalem and Athens," Cohen here presents the issue in terms of two different conceptual frameworks, both of which he has engaged in deeply: in one framework, God is ultimately understood not as a person but as a neuter or abstraction; in the other, by contrast, God is understood specifically as a person. This contrast between neuter/abstraction and person parallels Heschel's contrast between a what and a whom, and between an "it" and a "you," and it constitutes a key element in Cohen's presentation of Jewish religious thought and tradition.[21]

---

20 Cohen, Hermann, *Religion of Reason Out of the Sources of Judaism*, trans. Simon Kaplan, Atlanta, GA: Scholars Press, 1995, 42–43. See also Weiss, Daniel H., *Paradox and the Prophets: Hermann Cohen and the Indirect Communication of Religion*, New York: Oxford University Press, 2012, 142–143.

21 See also Heschel, "The God of Israel and Christian Renewal," 268: "The God of Israel is a 'devouring fire' (Deuteronomy 4:24), not an object of abstraction or generalization." Cohen likewise draws upon the contrast of "It" and "You," especially in the context of ethical relation to other human beings; see *Religion of Reason*, 14–16, and *Paradox and the Prophets*, 104–111, 122–123.

However, after asserting "Jewish religion's" transformation of God from a neuter into a person, Cohen also states, "As a result of this, admittedly, anthropomorphism becomes unavoidable."[22] Here, Cohen raises the concern that God's transcendent nature could seem to be lost by casting God as a person, in a manner analogous to the concerns about casting God as having a name: casting God in this way seems to be conceiving of God in categories that apply more properly to human beings, i.e., to created beings. While Cohen does not treat "God as person" as itself an instance of problematic anthropomorphism, he indicates that it simultaneously gives rise to an anthropomorphic tendency, which persistently accompanies this transformation from neuter to person and which structurally runs the risk of subsequently giving rise to problematic understandings of God. Yet, immediately after connecting "God as person" to concerns about anthropomorphism, Cohen adds, "the decline of Jewish thought into myth would have been unavoidable if the *fight against anthropomorphism* had not proved from the very beginning of the oral teaching to be the very soul of Jewish religious education. It is perhaps possible to say that this fight already played a role in the compilation of the Canon of Scripture. We do not, therefore, at this stage of our exposition need to take offense at the transformation of an abstraction into a person."[23] Cohen acknowledges concerns that "God as person" – as we saw earlier in relation to concerns about God having a name – could result in a problematic "decline into myth." Yet, Cohen simultaneously asserts that Jewish thought did *not* decline into myth, *even while* continuing to understand God as a person! Even if "God as a person" makes anthropomorphism "unavoidable," Jewish tradition was at the same time marked by an active fight against anthropomorphism, by a conscious effort to make sure that God's status as creator is distinguished from that of created human beings. Thus, despite what one might have thought, casting God as a person does *not* inevitably lead people who do so to lose sight of God's distinction from the created world, and in Cohen's assessment, the history of Jewish tradition constitutes a case in point. Instead, it is apparently possible, in practice, to understand and relate to God as a person – thus preserving an interpersonal relational dynamic between human beings and the creator of all – without declining into myth. In this regard, it is notable that Cohen describes this situation in terms of "the danger that is connected to the [notion of] the person."[24] Understanding God as a person thus gives rise to "danger" but does not constitute an inherent catastrophe. "God as person" is presented as something that can *potentially* lead a problematic decline into myth, but the latter is not a *necessary* consequence of the former. One

---

22 Cohen, *Religion of Reason*, 42, translation modified.
23 Cohen, *Religion of Reason*, 42–43, italics in the original.
24 Cohen, *Religion of Reason*, 43.

needs to be aware of the dangers and to make sure to actively combat them, but if one does so, one need not distance oneself from understanding God as a person. Given the connection, as we have seen, between "God as a person" and "God as having a name," Cohen's judgment would seem to apply to the latter as well: there may be a potential danger connected to the idea of God having a name, but this too is a danger that can be avoided by taking additional active steps to reemphasize God's status as creator, so that one likewise need not reject and can continue to uphold the idea of God having a name.

7 Wittgenstein's Clarifying Reflections

While Cohen's analysis points us to a potential means for addressing the problem of God's name, the specter of inconsistency still hovers over the issue. For this reason, we can now turn explicitly to Wittgenstein, whose broader reflections on the way words and language function, particularly in his *Philosophical Investigations*, can help us to see that the theological insistence that the creator of all cannot have a name shares important assumptions in common with many of the philosophical tendencies that Wittgenstein criticizes.

Consider the following paragraphs where Wittgenstein's imaginary interlocutor raises concerns in relation to issues of indefiniteness, vagueness, and blurriness:

a) Consider for example the proceedings that we call "games." I mean board-games, card-games, ball-games, Olympic games, and so on. What is common to them all? – Don't say: "There *must* be something common, or they would not be called 'games'" – but *look and see* whether there is anything common to all. – For if you look at them you will not see something that is common to *all*, but similarities, relationships, and a whole series of them at that. To repeat: don't think, but look! (*Philosophical Investigations* [hereafter *PI*] 66).

b) One might say that the concept 'game' is a concept with blurred edges. – "But is a blurred concept a concept at all?" – Is an indistinct photograph a picture of a person at all? Is it even always an advantage to replace an indistinct picture by a sharp one? Isn't the indistinct one often exactly what we need? (*PI* 71)

In *PI* 66, the imaginary interlocutor asserts that there "must" be something in common across the different activities we call "games." This insistence of "must," of unavoidable necessity, stems from a set assumption about how words function: namely, that there must be a "least common denominator" linking all instances of a given concept in order for the instances to properly be instances of that one concept. From this perspective, for any given term or concept, one will find it problematic if there does not appear to be any discoverable common denominator of this sort, and one must either work even harder to discover what that common denominator is; or, conversely, one must conclude that, if the different instances do *not* have a shared common denominator, then they must "really" be instances of multiple different concepts, which have mistakenly been assigned the same term due to the imperfect vagaries of everyday speech.

Opposing this framework, Wittgenstein calls into question the initial "must." Instead, he says: people do possess a concept of "game," i.e., they feel confident and comfortable using the term in conversation, and in general are not confused by its usage. When we look at different instances of the word "game," we find that they don't appear to share any single common denominator. From this, he draws a conclusion different from that of his interlocutor; he posits that because there does not appear to be a single common denominator for the term "game," then *at least some concepts* do not require a single common denominator in order to function. If there is not a single common denominator for all the different instances of "game," this need not mean that they cannot all properly be games, but rather that the concept "game" simply is one of those concepts whose operation does not contain a single common denominator.

Wittgenstein's call to "look and see" how the concept functions, rather than assume beforehand ("think"), is a key aspect in his method of "grammatical" investigation.[25] Crucial to this endeavor is the notion that various terms can have different "grammars" from other terms. Some terms may have closely related grammars ("The grammar of the word 'knows' is evidently closely related to that of 'can', 'is able to'." [*PI* 150]), while other terms may have divergent grammars ("This shows clearly that the grammar of 'to mean' is not like that of the expression 'to imagine' and the like." [*PI* 38]). With regard to the term "game," it may be that for certain other terms, it does seem more possible to name a common denominator among their various instances of the term's use. Some might therefore generalize from this and arrive at the assumption that *all* concepts must similarly have a common denominator. However, this generalization is not a necessary one and may in actual fact be unwarranted: without this generalizing assumption clouding our assessment, we would be in a better position to recognize that the concept of "game" does not operate with the same grammar as those other terms. In this case, the type of grammatical difference is linked to the question of an ap-

---

25 See *PI* 90, where Wittgenstein characterizes his basic investigatory method as "grammatical."

parent common denominator,[26] while in other cases, there could be other types of grammatical difference between any two given concepts. Thus, one should not assume that any given grammatical feature of a certain concept automatically applies to another concept; instead, one must always "look and see." As Wittgenstein emphasizes, "One cannot guess how a word functions. One has to look at its use and learn from that. But the difficulty is to remove the prejudice which stands in the way of doing this. It is not a stupid prejudice" (*PI* 340). Due to this "prejudice," various confusions can arise from working with a certain grammatical feature of one area of language, assuming it is inherently generalizable, then applying it to other areas of language and becoming puzzled when it seems not to fit. In a related context, Wittgenstein states, "We have only rejected the grammar which tries to force itself on us here. The paradox disappears only if we make a radical break with the idea that language always functions in one way, always serves the same purpose" (*PI* 304). In this formulation, Wittgenstein sympathizes with those who unwittingly apply the grammar from one area of language to another area of language. By saying that a certain grammar "tries to force itself on us here," he emphasizes that it can sometimes be difficult for people *not* to engage in the problematic mode of generalization, that it is an understandable tendency, even if it is not ultimately grounded or fruitful. But, if one can come to recognize that different areas of language can sometimes operate in different ways, with different grammatical features, then one will be in a better position to resist that generalizing tendency.

In *PI* 71 (as cited above), Wittgenstein engages further with his imaginary interlocutor regarding the concept "game," and he proposes to the interlocutor that one could potentially treat "game" as a concept "with blurred edges." In other words, using a visual metaphor, he suggests that if the notion of a shared common denominator corresponds to a visual figure with clear and sharp edges, then the concept "game" could be understood as a visual figure with blurred edges. It is not that the figure is completely blurry, but that its edges are blurred. Likewise, it is not that the different instances of "game" are completely different from one another, as there are many linkages between the different instances, but simply that there is no single shared element that fully unites all the instances. However, the interlocutor then protests, "But is a blurred concept a concept at all?" Here, the interlocutor is still working with the assumption that, in order to be a proper concept, it must be clear and distinct, corresponding to a common denominator

---

26 This need not mean that a term that *appears* to have a common denominator truly *does* have one that joins together *all* its uses; rather, the point is that some terms *at least seem* to have this property, and this is what gives rise to the generalizing assumption.

among all its instances. Wittgenstein responds by moving into a framing of value and desirability: "Is it even always an advantage to replace an indistinct picture by a sharp one? Isn't the indistinct one often exactly what we need?" In other words, it may be that the concept "game" is a very useful concept in our language *precisely because* it is versatile, linking together different instances don't *all* share a single common denominator. If one insisted that one could properly use only fully "sharp" concepts, one would thereby be cutting off a wide area of language-use. If one recognizes that the insistence on a shared common denominator is a contingent rather than a necessary requirement, one can appreciate the value for life and communication of concepts whose instances that don't share a single common denominator, and one need not view this as a problem to be solved or a paradox to be overcome. Rather, if one bases oneself on observation ("look and see"), one can view it as a normal feature of certain terms; the supposed "problem" arises only if you assume that "proper" concepts "must" operate with a shared common denominator.

Analogously, in relation to God's name, a certain approach could reason (as does Justin Martyr): if God were to have a name, this would make God a created being, since we know that for a being to have a name, that being *must* have been given that name by another being that preceded it. Hence, the creator of all cannot have a name. The "must" here is similar to the one examined above in relation to the concept "game." Just as it is understandable that some people could assume that for any concept, all instances of that concept must have a shared common denominator (since this *does* appear to be the case with many concepts), so too it is understandable to assume that having a name must go along with being a created being (since this *does* appear to be the case with most beings that have a name).

However, Wittgenstein's advice of "don't think, but look!" can apply here as well. If one "looks and sees," one can observe that the term game seems to work just fine as a communicative term in everyday life, and the fact that there is no apparent common denominator to all its instances does not generally appear to cause practical problems. To be sure, the absence of a common denominator could *in theory*, in certain situations, potentially lead to confusion. One could theoretically imagine someone familiar with ball-games being invited to play a card-game, and then asking, "Wait, but where is the ball? I thought we were going to play a *game*!" In practice, however, this sort of thing does not seem to be a frequent occurrence in relation to the term "game," and furthermore, if it did happen to occur, the misunderstanding could be easily corrected. Thus, there is no apparent need to reject "game" as a fully proper concept.

Now, it may be case that the type of confusion just described might be *less likely* to occur in relation to terms whose instances do more readily appear to have a common denominator. And if one wanted to eliminate even the theoretical possibility of this type of confusion, perhaps one would want to stick only to those latter type of concepts. But, the chance that there is a *greater* chance of confusion with concepts like "game" need not mean that there is a *high* chance of confusion, nor that such confusions could not be easily corrected in the off-chance that they did occur. Thus, the concern that Wittgenstein's interlocutor raises about "game" could also be described as allowing a theoretical anxiety to get in the way of recognizing that this is not something that one needs to worry about in actual practice and experience, and certainly not to the extent of avoiding using terms like "game." As an analogy, a person could refuse to step outside of their house out of anxiety that doing so will increase the chances that they would be eaten by a lion. And, such a person would even be correct in theory that going outside would indeed put one a greater risk of this potential danger. But, at least in many countries, if one takes proper care in what one does, particularly when, for example, visiting a zoo, this is very unlikely to happen, and at any rate is not something that most people would treat as a valid reason to never leave one's house.

Likewise, with regard to concerns about God having a name, one should "look and see" whether, in practice, understanding God as having a name is likely to lead to people treating God as a created being rather than as the creator. If it turns out that, in a given cultural-communal context, people are able to treat God as having a name *while also* keeping God's status as creator sharply distinguished from created beings, this calls into question the assumption that the former *must* undermine the latter.[27] The question of whether God having a name is problematic thus shifts from a theoretically-based concern to a practically-assessed one. While one could certainly imagine possibilities in which the idea of God having a name could lead to confusion – for instance, if someone were to conclude, "Ah, so some previous being must have given God God's name!" – it may be that in practice, a strong concurrent emphasis on God as the creator of all would make it less likely that someone would be led to draw such a conclusion. Furthermore, if one operates with the possibility of correction rather than solely depending on prevention, then one could also rectify such a misunderstanding if it did happen to occur. For example, one could respond, "That may be the case with most people's names, but that is not the case with God's name; God's name does not function with exactly the same grammar as do the names of human beings." Such a correc-

---

27 Such an assumption is equivalent to the position that a concept must "make sense" when reflected on in a logical-theoretical manner, or else we must judge it to be objectionable and in need of adjustment or reform.

tive addition can help to reinforce the fact that someone *could* draw the conclusion that someone must have given God God's name does not mean that one *must* draw such a conclusion.[28]

This latter assumption seems to be an instance of the type of phenomenon that Wittgenstein above called a "prejudice" concerning language and concepts, and that he elsewhere calls an "superstition" produced by "illusion": "this proves to be a superstition (not a mistake!), itself produced by grammatical illusions" (*PI* 110). If people are operating in a certain mode of thought, it can seem to them that the idea of God having a name would completely destroy and undermine God's status as creator, and they can provide coherent-sounding arguments why this must be the case. To say that this is a superstition rather than a mistake highlights the way in which this mindset can have the outward appearance of internal consistency. The illusory status of this conviction can mean that it is difficult simply to "think oneself out of it;" hence Wittgenstein's advice of "don't think, but look!"[29] While Wittgenstein recognizes that it can be difficult to break away from

---

28 Wittgenstein repeatedly emphasizes, particularly in relation to religious issues, that one need not always draw certain conclusions, even if such conclusions *could* appear to "logically" follow. Instead, to understand a concept, one needs to look and see what conclusions a person *does* in fact draw. See, e.g, his comments in his *Lectures and Conversations on Aesthetics, Psychology and Religious Belief*, Berkeley: University of California Press, 1966: "If he says this, I won't know yet what consequences he will draw. I don't know what he opposes this to." (69) "I meant: what conclusions are you going to draw? Etc Are eyebrows going to be talked of, in connection with the eye of God." (71) "When I say he's using a picture, I'm merely making a *grammatical* remark: [What I say] can only be verified by the consequences he does or does not draw" (72); "On the other hand, you may not wish to draw any such consequences, and this is all there is to it – except further muddles" (72). See also Arif Ahmed's formulation of Wittgenstein's general approach, in which "the *possibility* of deriving a contradiction from certain rules does not make those rules unusable if we do not *in fact* derive the contradiction." See Ahmed, *Wittgenstein's 'Philosophical Investigations': A Reader's Guide*, London: Continuum, 2010, 55.
29 When Wittgenstein says this in relation to the concept "game" and its various instances, he is primarily combating the tendency for people to say "There *must* be something common, or they would not be called 'games.'" In other words, they assume that the concept "game" is a legitimate concept, and conclude that therefore there must be a common denominator among its instances. However, the same tendency could also give rise to a different but related response to the situation: namely, a person could say: "I have looked carefully at the different instances of the term 'game', and I am unable to find a common denominator. Therefore, there must be something problematic or confused about our concept 'game', and we need to replace it by one or more different concepts, each of which has a clear common denominator." (Cf. Wittgenstein's response to this way of thinking in, e.g., *PI* 98: "[W]e are not *striving after* an ideal, as if our ordinary vague sentences had not yet got a quite unexceptional vague sense, and a perfect language awaited construction by us." See also *PI* 81, 100, 132.) This latter response would still be afflicted by the same type of "illusion" as the first, i.e., both responses assume that any proper concept

this type of assumption, he nevertheless views it as having a detrimental effect on people's lives and on their understanding of other human beings. He writes, "We mind about the kind of expressions we use concerning these things; we do not understand them, however, but misinterpret them. When we do philosophy we are like savages, primitive people, who hear the expressions of civilized men, put a false interpretation on them, and then draw the queerest conclusions from it" (*PI* 194). Here, Wittgenstein draws upon the problematic tropes of "primitive" and "civilized," but does so in order to reverse typical assumptions about who is "primitive." A certain mode of philosophizing (or philosophical theologizing) assumes that certain conceptions – for example, the idea that the creator of all has a name – are "backwards" and "primitive," and that the "civilized" and "advanced" understanding is the one that can recognize that the creator of all must be nameless. By contrast, Wittgenstein asserts that it is those who take this latter stance who in fact lack the ability to properly interpret and construe the ideas of others, and who cast such ideas as gravely problematic when, in fact, this judgment itself stems from a type of superstition, prejudice, and illusion. The "illusory" element is not the view that the creator of all is nameless, but rather the view that the creator of all *must be* nameless.[30] This leads those who are under this illusion to denigrate and dismiss ways of understanding various concepts that, in reality, need not be treated as objectionable. Thus, if one can free oneself from illusions of this "must," it can turn out that, in practice, one can uphold the notion of God's name – and the elements of interpersonal address, prayer, and relation that it carries – without thereby placing God in the category of created beings.

To be sure, there will still remain a certain tension or ambiguity in upholding the idea that the creator of all also has a name. For instance, it may give rise to questions with no readily available answer, such as, "Where did God's name

---

must have a common denominator among its instances. In the case of God's name, the objections tend to be more like the second type of "illusory" response: "When I think about this idea, I can't find a way of logically combining 'name' and 'creator of all.' Therefore, there is something problematic about the idea of God having a name, and we must replace it by an understanding of God as nameless." By contrast, one can "look and see" that many of our everyday concepts, when subjected to pure theoretical reflection, do not lend themselves to full logical consistency, but that this "deficiency" should not in itself be treated as sufficient cause for deeming those concepts objectionable.

30 Likewise, it is not a superstition, prejudice, or illusion to note that "name" (or "individual," or "person," etc.) can be seen as *standing in a type of tension with* "creator of all." Both Heschel and Cohen, for instance, recognize such a tension. Rather, the superstitious or illusory part lies in the insistence that we must eliminate such tensions from our concepts in order for them to be properly legitimate, and that a concept that retains such a tension is necessarily objectionable and inferior to a concept that has eliminated this tension.

come from then?"[31] This could be analogous to someone continuing to insist, "But *how can* the term 'game' really work as a concept if there isn't a common denominator? There must be one, I just can't seem to figure out what it is!" The ambiguity that remains around God's name could lead some people to insist that we must declare that God must be nameless. While this is one possible response that would indeed resolve the ambiguity, it can structurally impair personal relation with God as a "you," and so may constitute an undesirably Procrustean "solution."[32] Instead, one can face the ambiguity or tension involved with God's name, while emphasizing that this is not a practically problematic tension, since in practice one can easily maintain God's status as creator without any major difficulty, despite the tension that remains if one reflects theoretically on the issue.[33]

---

31 It may well be that a question like this is one that various types of people (and not just philosophers) could raise, and that talking about God having a name could indeed contribute to such questions being raised, since it *is* the case that, for most of the named individuals we encounter, there *was* someone else who preceded them and gave them their name. The problematic element comes not in the raising of such questions, but in feeling that you *need* an answer that will resolve the tension.

32 Importantly, the opposite type of Procrustean resolution of the tension can be equally problematic. If the one approach resolved the tension by removing the seemingly "immanent" aspects of God (in this case, the idea of God having a name), the other approach could resolve the tension by removing the seemingly transcendent aspects. See, for example, James Diamond, who, in rightly criticizing abstract-transcendent construals of "God as Being," may incline a bit too far in the direction of immanence by presenting God as a "God of becoming." See Diamond, *Jewish Theology Unbound*, Oxford: Oxford University Press, 2018, esp. chapter 3, "Naming an Unnamable God: Divine Being or Divine Becoming." On the risks of over-immanence in comparison to the risks of over-transcendence, see, e.g., Burrell, David, "Does Process Theology Rest on a Mistake?", *Theological Studies* 43 (1982), 125–135.

33 In other words, it can be fine or even natural that people may feel a certain type of "confusion" if they reflect on the conjunction of "name" and "creator of all." While this conceptual tension may not be able to be fully "resolved," it may also be that it is not a tension that needs or ought to be resolved. In Wittgenstein's treatment of the concept "game," his interlocutor expresses a concern that the different instances of "game" do not appear to have a common denominator, and this observation is linked to anxiety and confusion for the interlocutor. Importantly, in proposing that one can think of "game" in relation to "family resemblance" rather than "common denominator," Wittgenstein is *not* seeking to fully resolve the tension discerned by the interlocutor. Rather, if one "presses hard" on 'family resemblance,' one will find that this too does not provide full theoretical clarity regarding the concept "game." Instead, Wittgenstein proposes this framing as a heuristic way of coaxing the interlocutor to recognize that various concepts can be legitimate even if they do not lend themselves to a certain type of theoretical clarity. The concept "game" will retain a certain type of theoretical tension and when one reflects on it, and will still not fully "make sense" in this regard, regardless of whether one frames it in terms of "family resemblance" or "common denominator" – but the presence of this type of theoretical tension is not inherently problematic, but is a natural feature of many (if not all) of our everyday concepts,

Put differently, one can say that the sense that there is something problematic about "God having a name" is justified – there *is* something "problematic" about this idea, insofar as it could in principle lead some people into problematically losing sight of God's status as creator of all, if they were to conclude that a preexisting someone else must have given God God's name, as is the case with other named beings. But, while this is a potential problem, it is not the case that people necessarily *will actually* be led to such problematic conclusions simply by encountering the tradition of God's name. At the same time, one can also say that assertions that God is nameless are *also* problematic, and can lead to different types of problems and confusions. For example, such an assertion could have negative effects on a person's ability to relate personally to God: "If God is nameless, is this the type of God that I can pray to and address as a 'you'?" If one is less concerned about prayer and relation to God, one might be inclined to focus on the problems that can arise from God having a name, and might be inclined to solve the problem by abandoning or "progressing beyond" that idea. However, if one is more concerned about prayer and relation to God, then one might be more concerned about the problems that can arise from asserting God to be nameless. If we recognize that there is something problematic about God having a name *and* something problematic about God being nameless, then there is no avoiding some type of problem, and the judgment about which problem is more concerning (or more likely to create problems in actual practical terms) must be resolved on the basis of something other than "logical necessity." At the very least, the idea of God having a name is no longer inherently more problematic than the idea of God as nameless, and it may be that the former is more suited, in practice, to retaining together both God's status as creator *and* personal relation to God.[34]

---

even though this tension may be more readily apparent in relation to some concepts (such as "game") than to others. There could be *some* types of theoretical tension that do indicate something problematic, but the mere presence of theoretical tension is not in itself warrant for deeming a concept to be problematic or as requiring resolution; rather, it is important to recognize that at least certain types of "conceptual unclarity" don't need or call for "resolving."

34 Indeed, it could even be argued that God as having a name could actually *help* in preserving God's differentiation from created beings. As Heschel notes in the quotation cited above, "A notion you can conceive; a name you call." Relating to God as having a name can help for reinforcing the notion that God is not reducible to a notion that can be conceived, and can thus help for resisting tendencies to turn God into a "conceptual object." In this sense, God as named can be linked to upholding God's otherness and transcendence – the type of otherness that accompanies relating to another as a "you" rather than as an "it." Similarly, Soulen ("'Go Tell Pharaoh,' or Why Empires Prefer a Nameless God") draws out related ethical-political implications of upholding the idea of God as having a name. (I am grateful to conversation with Darren Frey for helping to draw out the ideas in this footnote and paragraph.)

An analogy can be drawn to the maintenance of plants. It is the case that growing live plants requires a certain amount of care, such as regular watering and weeding. In this context, if one neglects that maintenance, there is a chance that the plants will wither and die. Thus, a certain element of tension is structurally part of maintaining live plants: one must remain consciously attuned to ways in which one's efforts could "go wrong." Some people could therefore conclude: in order to avoid the chance of the plants withering and dying, let us just switch to plastic plants, which don't require that type of active maintenance. Likewise, one can choose between understandings of God that don't need any "watering" but which are lacking in various otherwise desirable qualities – or, you can make use of concepts that can sometimes require some care or correction, but can provide for richer forms of communal life and relation to God. And, as Wittgenstein shows, just as people who are accustomed and habituated to how the term "game" is used can do so without difficulty, so too it turns out that the idea of God as creator and as having a name can be readily upheld in practice without undermining either of those two commitments.

These reflections can provide a fuller understanding of Wittgenstein's otherwise-brief remark in which he states, "Luther said that theology is the grammar of the word 'God.' I interpret this to mean that an investigation of the word would be a grammatical one." What does it mean to investigate the word "God" in a "grammatical" way, and how would this approach be different from other approaches to "doing theology"? A grammatical approach to the word "God" would appear to involve a "look and see" orientation: within a given cultural-communal context, is God treated as having a name, and is God also treated as the creator of all? Are these two elements both employed without generating practical difficulties? If so, then theological reflection in a grammatical mode could then say: apparently, in this tradition, God is properly understood in relation to both of these elements. There may be certain things that *are* treated in this tradition as incompatible with God as creator of all, but apparently having a name is not one of those things. The assertion of God as creator of all may place certain constraints on *how one understands* the fact that God has a name, but it is apparently not seen as incompatible with that fact in itself.

This approach to theology stands in contrast to an approach more linked to the "think" orientation that Wittgenstein opposes in saying "Don't think, but look!" The less "grammatical" approach would be more inclined to say something like: "We can see by logical deduction that having a name is something that inherently marks a being as created rather than as the creator. Thus, I don't care if in this or that cultural context people say that God has a name while also claiming that God is the creator of all. This only shows that those people are conceptually confused and have not progressed to the recognition that God, as creator, *must* be nameless. Furthermore, I'm also not so concerned about whether the idea of God having a name causes practical problems in relation to upholding God as creator; maybe it does or maybe it doesn't, but we must reject the idea of God as having a name since the two elements are simply logically incompatible. The conceptual conjunction of the two just doesn't 'make sense,' logically speaking." In this mode, a key task of theology is sorting through the existing ways of talking and "smoothing out" the apparent logical inconsistencies and ambiguities in order to arrive at a properly "distinct picture" of how to understand God.

By contrast, the grammatical approach holds open the possibility that certain understandings of God may contain theoretical ambiguities that one should not seek to "fully clarify," since in some cases, the equivalent of an "indistinct picture" might be "exactly what we need," e.g., in enabling us to uphold God's distinction from created beings while also enabling personal relation to God as a "you." Thus, while various types of conceptual ambiguity or tension could potentially be problematic and call for a means of overcoming them, at least some elements of conceptual tension may be *desirable* in various cases in order to properly preserve, convey, and reinforce certain ideas. Thus, the seemingly "strange" rabbinic "grammar of the God's name" can point not to a deficient or insufficiently thought-out understanding, but to a fully robust understanding of a *different concept* that differs in important ways from a "nameless God" and which need not be forced into a different framework on the grounds of "logical necessity" or "theoretical consistency."[35]

In a grammatical approach to theology, one would judge certain ideas to be problematic by looking and seeing whether certain things that you're saying are in actual fact and practice causing problems in relation to other things you'd want to uphold. In other words, if, in a given communal context and a given time and place, talking about God as having a name *did* have a strong tendency to lead people to relate to God as a created being, then this would be grounds for saying that there is a *problematic* conflict between these two elements.[36] But, this would be a question to be checked empirically, and not simply assessed on the basis of whether someone *could theoretically* draw problematic conclusions from the idea

---

35 Cf. Heschel, "The God of Israel and Christian Renewal," 271: "[The God of Israel] means God with whom Israel is vitally, intimately involved, and involvement transcending the realm of thinking, not reducible to human consistency, and one which does not simplify itself in order to accommodate common sense."

36 Again, the question of whether there is a problematic or objectionable conflict between two elements is not the same as the question of whether one can discern a conceptual tension between two elements. The latter could be the case without the former being the case, and this may in fact be the case with many of our everyday concepts, even if this internal tension is more readily apparent in the case of some concepts than of others.

of God having a name. If a concept can't be "maintained" without creating grave problems, then that does properly make it a problem in a stronger sense – but if one can pass down and transmit the concept without it leading to problematic understandings, then it should not be treated as deficient or in need of correction.[37]

Thus, if we consider the classical rabbinic approaches to God's name alongside Justin Martyr's approach, we can see that while both of them reflect on and interpret the text of the Hebrew Bible, they appear to incline toward different modes of "theologizing." The classical rabbinic texts (as well as the texts of the New Testament, as argued by Soulen) seem not to be bothered by the idea that God has a name, and they do not seem to feel compelled to eliminate the biblical text's apparent naming of God when they present their own theological understanding. This appears more in keeping with a "grammatical" approach to theologizing. By contrast, Justin seems more concerned to insist that the creator of all – by force of logic – cannot have a name, such that all the *apparent* namings of God in the biblical text, when properly understood, are in fact "not names, but appellations derived from His good deeds and functions." His approach, in this regard, seems more like the non-grammatical mode of theologizing that feels more compelled to eliminate apparent logical inconsistencies in the manner we have described above. While one need not create an absolute dichotomy between Justin's approach and that of the rabbis, it does seem clear that Justin's approach is at least *more* shaped by this type of desire to eliminate logical-theoretical ambiguity from his understanding of God.[38]

This assessment gains further reinforcement when we consider Justin's approach to God's communication with human beings. As emphasized by Heschel,

---

37 In discussing "theology as the grammar of the word 'God,'" Wittgenstein further notes: "What is ridiculous or blasphemous also shows the grammar of the word" (*Wittgenstein's Lectures, Cambridge 1932–1935*, ed. Alice Ambrose, Blackwell: Oxford, 1979, 32). These judgments, though, may differ between different communities: what one community finds ridiculous or blasphemous may be judged as unproblematic by another community, and thus would not stand in need of correction in the latter theological framework.

38 Just as Justin may be further away from the "grammatical" approach than the New Testament is, so likewise some subsequent Jewish thinkers – e.g., Maimonides – may be further away from the "grammatical" approach than the classical rabbinic texts are. See Weiss, Daniel H. "The God of the Intellect and the God of Lived Religion(s): Reflections on Maimonides, Wittgenstein and Burrell," in: Gorazd Andrejč/Daniel H. Weiss (eds.), *Interpreting Interreligious Relations with Wittgenstein: Philosophy, Theology and Religious Studies*, Brill: Boston, 2019, 174–193. Note, however, that Maimonides, while reshaping many aspects of God to fit with certain philosophical positions similar to Justin's, still does retain the idea of the Tetragrammaton as God's proper name! See Fagenblat, Michael, *A Covenant of Creatures: Levinas's Philosophy of Judaism*, Stanford: Stanford University Press, 2010, 123–130.

the notion of God having a name is closely linked to understanding God and human individuals as standing in a direct, intimate, and interpersonal mode of relation and communication with one another. If these two elements are connected, and if Justin expresses concern about the notion of the creator of all having a name, then we might expect him also to express similar concerns about direct communication between the transcendent creator of all and earthly human beings. Thus, Justin asserts that "the senseless Jews" think that the one who spoke to Moses out of the burning bush in Exodus was "the Father and Creator of the universe."[39] However, by holding this opinion, the Jews show themselves to be in error, and stand under the rebuking judgment of Isaiah 1:3, where the prophet declares, "Israel doth not know Me, my people have not understood Me."[40] Justin states those with a proper understanding would recognize that it was not the Father who spoke to Moses out of the burning Bush, but rather the Son, who "is sent forth" by the Father to declare whatever is revealed.[41] Furthermore, he states more generally about the biblical books, that "wherever God says, (. . .) 'The Lord spoke to Moses,'" the text is referring specifically to the Son as the speaker and not the Father.[42] What is notable about Justin's approach is not that he happens to interpret the text as referring to the Son and not the Father; the notable aspect is his *reason* that he gives for interpreting the text in this way: describing "the ineffable Father and Lord of All," Justin asserts that "He is not moved or confined to a spot in the whole world, for He existed before the world was made. How, then, could He talk with any one (. . .)?"[43] It is God's transcendent, uncreated, and unmovable nature that marks the idea of the Father speaking to Moses, or to any human being, as a fundamental impossibility and misunderstanding of God; hence, all the biblical texts that might seem to imply otherwise must be reinterpreted as referring to the Son. Anyone who thinks otherwise – and he indicates that "the Jews" do think that "the Father and Creator of the Universe" did speak to Moses – show themselves to be "senseless." In this, Justin displays an orientation similar to his theologizing about the impossibility of creator of all having a name.

By contrast, the classical rabbinic texts do not seem to have a problem with the idea that the creator of all spoke to Moses, without the need for an intermediary or mediator, similarly to the way they do not seem to have a problem with the idea that the creator of all has a name. They do not view such direct interpersonal com-

39 Justin Martyr, *First Apology*, 63.
40 Justin Martyr, *First Apology*, 63.
41 Justin Martyr, *First Apology*, 63; see also Justin Martyr, *Dialogue with Trypho*, 59–60.
42 Justin Martyr, *Dialogue with Trypho*, 127.
43 Justin Martyr, *Dialogue with Trypho*, 127.

munication as undermining God's distinction from creation and status as creator.[44] And, while they do not see human beings today as receiving the type of prophetic communication that Moses received from God, the fact that such communication is compatible with God's status serves to undergird their sense that human beings today can relate to the creator of all directly in prayer.[45] For Justin, on the other hand, it appears that such unmediated relation to the Father does not make sense; hence he states that the member of the worshipping community that presides over the Eucharist "gives praise and glory to the Father of the universe, through the name of the Son and of the Holy Ghost"[46] and that "We bless the Maker of all through His Son Jesus Christ, and through the Holy Ghost."[47] There is an internal consistency in Justin's insistence that one conveys praise, glory and blessing to the (nameless) Father not directly, but through the (name-having) Son.[48] This particular form of consistency, however, seems to be something that the rabbinic texts do not

---

44 As noted above in fn 12, their stance need not be seen as the result of philosophical naïveté, as though they were simply blissfully ignorant of the type of concerns raised by Justin and by others influenced by a similar metaphysical framework. Rather, the cultural context of the classical rabbis would likely have made them well-aware of such objections, so that their continued emphasis on direct human relation to the "creator of all" should be seen as a conscious and deliberate choice. On rabbinic engagement with their broader cultural context, see, e.g., Lieberman, Saul, "How Much Greek in Jewish Palestine?" in: Alexander Altmann (ed.), *Biblical and Other Studies*, 123–141, Cambridge: Harvard University Press, 1963; Hidary, Richard, *Rabbis and Classical Rhetoric: Sophistic Education and Oratory in the Talmud and Midrash*, Cambridge: Cambridge University Press, 2018.

45 In this regard, they may be drawing upon biblical texts such as Ex. 33:11 ("The LORD would speak to Moses face to face, as one speaks to a friend," as well as on texts that extend this direct relating to the entire Israelite community (e.g., Deut. 5:4: "The LORD talked with you face to face in the mount out of the midst of the fire").

46 Justin Martyr, *First Apology*, 65.

47 Justin Martyr, *First Apology*, 67.

48 It may be that Justin's assigning of name-having to the Son rather than the Father may not satisfactorily resolve the philosophical problem of "God having a name," particularly for later Christian theologians who, in a subsequent Nicene Christian theological context, seek to assign "fully equal divinity" to the Son as well as the Father. That is to say, Justin himself held a conception in which "the logos was not eternal in the later Nicene sense" (Barnard, Leslie William, *Justin Martyr: His Life and Thought*, London: Cambridge University Press, 1966, 90). As such, within Justin's own framework, assigning a name to the non-eternal Son/logos may be less problematic; however, those who do want to say that the Son is "eternal in the later Nicene sense" may find that the idea of the Son having a name raises problems similar to those raised by the idea of the Father having a name.

By contrast, one can view the rabbinic texts as "grasping the nettle" of the seeming problem by simply saying that the creator of all also has a name. In this regard, as discussed above in relation to Soulen's analysis (see fns 6, 10–11 above), many texts in the New Testament may be more similar to the rabbinic approach in their affirmation of God having a name.

see as necessary in their account of relation to God, and thus affirm that human beings can relate directly to the (name-having) creator of all.

Finally, we can reflect on the way in which the rabbinic approach, which appears to more closely align with Wittgenstein's "grammatical" approach to theologizing, can also be understood as displaying a sensitivity to the unresolved tension and ambiguity linked to the idea that the creator of all has a name. The rabbinic approach, while wanting to retain the idea of God's name for reasons already discussed, may also sense that the act of everyday human beings (apart from the high priest in the special setting of the Temple) addressing God by God's name could indeed impinge upon God's sovereignty and transcendent authority as an act of *lèse-majesté*: not that it is *logically* impossible to address God by name, but that it is *ethically* and *religiously* inappropriate to do so. Thus, by saying that God has a name (as written in the scriptural text), but that we (currently) address God in prayer with the special substitute-name of *Adonai*, the rabbinic approach enables direct and intimate address to God in prayer as a "you" with a name, while keeping in place a form of restraint that enacts an attitude of piety and respect.[49] Seen from this perspective, those who discern a tension in the idea of the creator of all having a name are not completely incorrect, but they are led to an unhelpful elimination of God's name when they *logicize* this tension instead of *ethicizing* it. Moreover, the rabbinic approach, which aligns more with the latter, deals with the tension not by seeking to eliminate it but rather by preserving and respecting it. In this way, it can function as a core element of a form of religious life that works in practice to preserve both the intimacy and personal relation linked to the idea of God having a name *alongside* the respect and transcendence appropriate to God as creator of all.[50]

8 Conclusion

The different stances displayed by classical rabbinic literature and Justin Martyr are not merely a thing of the past, as there are many theologically-engaged people today who would still view the idea of God having a specific name as inherently problematic, and would be more inclined to judge Justin's approach to be is a bet-

---

49 At the same time, the rabbinic affirmation that legitimate pronunciation of God's name took place in the past and will take place again in the messianic future helps keep the "you"-aspects of God's name more salient, even in a time when there is currently no legitimate context for pronouncing God's name. That is, God not only has a name in theory, but also in human practice, even if that practice is not legitimately available in the current era.

50 Cf. Max Kadushin's analysis of rabbinic prayer as "normal mysticism" in his *Worship and Ethics: A Study in Rabbinic Judaism*, Binghamton: Global Publications, 2001 [1963], 163–198.

ter one, and to view the rabbinic preservation of God's name as a backwards vestige that ought rightly to be overcome. But, aided by Wittgenstein, we have seen that this stance may stem from a failure to assess whether the idea is necessarily problematic or objectionable when considered in practice, and may be more shaped by the illusory "must" that he sees as afflicting various philosophical problems.

Such illusions can lead some to reject or condemn things that they might otherwise acknowledge as having value and benefit. Many of those who reject the idea of God's name might say, "Yes, I agree that perhaps the idea of God having a name *could* augment the personal-relational quality of religious life and worship – sadly, however, it is simply something we must forgo if we want to preserve the idea of God as creator." By contrast, Wittgenstein's analysis helps us to see that such a conclusion is not in fact necessary. If one truly thinks that one's religious life would be improved by understanding God as nameless, then one is at liberty to do so, but one should not do so out of an assumption that this *must* be the case in order for God to remain distinct from created beings.

Viewed in this light, the rabbinic texts need no longer come across as "philosophically unsophisticated" but may instead reflect an implicit "grammatical" orientation to theologizing that is more akin to Wittgenstein's recognition that *not all things* that some philosophical approaches *claim* as "grave problems" ought appropriately to be treated as such. Based on this type of critical reassessment, further engagement with the rabbinic texts can function as a useful tool for identifying problems that affect various types of theologizing today, both in relation to the particular issue of God's name, and in relation to a wider range of theological "problems," not only in the context of Jewish tradition but also in the related theological frameworks of Christian and Islamic tradition. As Wittgenstein's concern that "A picture held us captive" (*PI* 115) appears to apply to theological as well as philosophical reflection, his recommendation of "grammatical" investigations can therefore helpfully aid in freeing us from that captivity and releasing us from unnecessary burdens and anxieties in relation to the word "God."[51]

51 I thank Genia Schönbaumsfeld, Farid Suleiman, and Mira Sievers for helpful comments on earlier versions of this essay.

Bibliography

Ahmed, Arif, *Wittgenstein's 'Philosophical Investigations': A Reader's Guide*, London: Continuum, 2010.

Barnard, Leslie William, *Justin Martyr: His Life and Thought*, London: Cambridge University Press, 1966.

Ben-Sasson, Hillel, *Understanding YHWH: The Name of God in Biblical, Rabbinic, and Medieval Jewish Thought*, London: Palgrave Macmillan, 2019.

Burrell, David, "Does Process Theology Rest on a Mistake?" *Theological Studies* 43 (1982), 125–135.

Cohen, Hermann, *Religion of Reason Out of the Sources of Judaism*, trans. Simon Kaplan, Atlanta, GA: Scholars Press, 1995.

Diamond, James, *Jewish Theology Unbound*, Oxford: Oxford University Press, 2018.

Fagenblat, Michael, *A Covenant of Creatures: Levinas's Philosophy of Judaism*, Stanford: Stanford University Press, 2010.

Hayes, Christine, "Displaced Self-Perceptions: The Deployment of Minim and Romans in b. Sanhedrin 90b–91a," in: Hayim Lapin (ed.), *Religious and Ethnic Communities in Later Roman Palestine*, 249–289, Bethesda: University Press of Maryland, 1998.

Heschel, Abraham Joshua, *God in Search of Man: A Philosophy of Judaism*, New York: Farrar, Straus, and Giroux, 1976.

Heschel, Abraham Joshua, *Moral Grandeur and Spiritual Audacity*, ed. Susannah Heschel, New York: Farrar, Straus, and Giroux, 1996.

Heschel, Abraham Joshua, *The Prophets*, New York: Perennial, 2001.

Hidary, Richard, *Rabbis and Classical Rhetoric: Sophistic Education and Oratory in the Talmud and Midrash*, Cambridge: Cambridge University Press, 2018.

Justin Martyr, *Ante-Nicene Fathers*, vol. 1, ed. Alexander Roberts/James Donaldson,/A. Cleveland Coxe, Buffalo: Christian Literature Publishing Co., 1885.

Kadushin, Max, *Worship and Ethics: A Study in Rabbinic Judaism*, Binghamton: Global Publications, 2001 [1963].

Kadushin, Max, *The Rabbinic Mind*, Binghamton: Global Publications, 2001 [1972].

Labendz, Jenny, *Socratic Torah: Non-Jews in Rabbinic Intellectual Culture*, Oxford: Oxford University Press, 2013.

Lieberman, Saul, "How Much Greek in Jewish Palestine?" in: Alexander Altmann (ed.), *Biblical and Other Studies*, 123–141, Cambridge: Harvard University Press, 1963.

Lorberbaum, Yair, *In God's Image: Myth, Theology, and Law in Classical Judaism*, Cambridge: Cambridge University Press, 2015.

Rosenzweig, Franz, *God, Man and the World: Lectures and Essays*, ed. and trans. Barbara Galli, Syracuse: Syracuse University Press, 1998.

Soulen, Kendall, *The Divine Name(s) and the Holy Trinity: Distinguishing the Voices*, Louisville: Westminster John Knox Press, 2011.

Soulen, Kendall, "'Go Tell Pharaoh,' or Why Empires Prefer a Nameless God," in: Jürgen Moltmann/ Timothy Eberhart/Matthew W. Charlton (eds.), *The Economy of Salvation: Essays in Honour of M. Douglas Meeks*, 58–70, Eugene: Cascade, 2015.

Soulen, Kendall, "Jesus and the Divine Name," *Union Seminary Quarterly Review* 65, no.1–2 (2015), 47–58.

Soulen, Kendall, *Irrevocable: The Name of God and the Unity of the Christian Bible*, Minneapolis: Fortress Press, 2022.

Stern, David, "*Imitatio Hominis*: Anthropomorphism and the Character(s) of God in Rabbinic Literature," *Prooftexts* 12, no. 2 (1992), 151–174.

Weiss, Daniel H., "The God of the Intellect and the God of Lived Religion(s): Reflections on Maimonides, Wittgenstein and Burrell," in: Gorazd Andrejč/Daniel H. Weiss (eds.), *Interpreting Interreligious Relations with Wittgenstein: Philosophy, Theology and Religious Studies*, 174–193, Brill: Boston, 2019.

Weiss, Daniel H., *Paradox and the Prophets: Hermann Cohen and the Indirect Communication of Religion*, New York: Oxford University Press, 2012.

Wettstein, Howard, *The Significance of Religious Experience*, New York: Oxford University Press, 2012.

Wittgenstein, Ludwig, *Lectures and Conversations on Aesthetics, Psychology and Religious Belief*, Berkeley: University of California Press, 1966.

Wittgenstein, Ludwig, *Wittgenstein's Lectures, Cambridge 1932–1935*, ed. Alice Ambrose, Blackwell: Oxford, 1979.

Wittgenstein, Ludwig, *Philosophical Investigations*, ed. G. E. M. Anscombe/Peter M. S. Hacker/Joachim Schulte, Chichester, West Sussex, U.K/Malden, MA: Wiley-Blackwell,[4]2010.

Suggestions for Further Reading

Ben-Sasson, Hillel, *Understanding YHWH: The Name of God in Biblical, Rabbinic, and Medieval Jewish Thought*, London: Palgrave Macmillan, 2019.

Cherbonnier, Edmond, "The Logic of Biblical Anthropomorphism," *Harvard Theological Review* 55, no. 3 (1962), 187–206.

Heschel, Abraham Joshua, *The Prophets*, New York: Perennial, 2001.

Kadushin, Max, *The Rabbinic Mind*, Binghamton: Global Publications, 2001 [1972].

Lorberbaum, Yair, *In God's Image: Myth, Theology, and Law in Classical Judaism*, Cambridge: Cambridge University Press, 2015.

Rosenzweig, Franz, "A Note on Anthropomorphisms: in Response to the Encyclopedia Judaica's Article" [1928], in his *God, Man and the World: Lectures and Essays*, ed. and trans. Barbara Galli, Syracuse: Syracuse University Press, 1998, 135–45.

Soulen, Kendall, *The Divine Name(s) and the Holy Trinity: Distinguishing the Voices*, Louisville: Westminster John Knox Press, 2011.

Stern, David, "*Imitatio Hominis*: Anthropomorphism and the Character(s) of God in Rabbinic Literature," *Prooftexts* 12, no. 2 (1992), 151–74.

Weiss, Daniel H., "The God of the Intellect and the God of Lived Religion(s): Reflections on Maimonides, Wittgenstein and Burrell," in: Gorazd Andrejč/Daniel H. Weiss (eds.), *Interpreting Interreligious Relations with Wittgenstein: Philosophy, Theology and Religious Studies*, 174–93, Brill: Boston, 2019.

Wettstein, Howard, *The Significance of Religious Experience*, New York: Oxford University Press, 2012.

Farid Suleiman
The Grammar of "God" – Muslim Perspectives

1 Introduction

The so-called "Dream Argument" by René Descartes (d. 1650), as most students of Western philosophy know, calls into question the reality of everything that we take for granted, including the existence of our bodies.[1] What is less known is that Descartes' source of inspiration for this argument might have been the famous Muslim theologian Abū Ḥāmid al-Ghazālī (d. 1111/504), who argued in a quite similar way that all what we perceive as real may in fact be nothing else but dream appearances.[2] In his work *al-Munqidh min aḍ-ḍalāl* (The Deliverer from Error), he writes:[3]

> Do you not see (. . .) how, when you are asleep, you believe things and imagine circumstances, holding them to be stable and enduring, and, so long as you are in that dream-condition, have no doubts about them? And is it not the case that when you awake you know that all you have imagined and believed is unfounded and ineffectual? Why then are you confident that all your waking beliefs, whether from sense or intellect, are genuine? They are true in respect of your present state; but it is possible that a state will come upon you whose relation to your waking consciousness is analogous to the relation of the latter to dreaming. In comparison with this state your waking consciousness would be like dreaming!

The argument seems so attractive because it relates to ordinary experiences that many can identify with. If we could be (and really are) wrong in some cases,

---

1 Descartes, René, *Oeuvres De Descartes. Nouvelle Présentation*, ed. Charles Adam/Paul Tannery, 11 vols, Paris: J. Vrin, 1982–91, 7; 19.
2 The striking similarity between al-Ghazālī's and Descartes' "dream argument" has led to a debate on whether the former actually influenced the latter. For a summary see López-Farjeat, Luis Xavier, "al-Ghazālī on Knowledge ('ilm) and Certainty (yaqīn) in al-Munqidh min aḍ-Ḍalāl and al-Qisṭās al-Mustaqīm," in: Georges Tamer (ed.), *Islam and Rationality: The Impact of Al-Ghazālī. Papers Collected on His 900th Anniversary*, vol. 1, 229–252, Leiden/Boston: Brill, 2015, 232, fn. 8. López-Farjeat writes that while there is no evidence that Descartes had direct access to the relevant work of al-Ghazālī, there are plausible other ways of how Descartes could have come to know about its content. See also Rudolph, Ulrich (ed.), *Philosophie in der islamischen Welt: 11. und 12. Jahrhundert: Zentrale und östliche Gebiete*, Basel: Schwabe Verlag, 2021, 294; 334.
3 Watt, William M., *The Faith and Practice of Al-Ghazālī*, London: George Allen and Unwin, 1953, 24.

Acknowledgements: I wish to express my gratitude to Genia Schönbaumsfeld, Daniel Weiss and Mira Sievers for their valuable input on a previous draft of this essay.

https://doi.org/10.1515/9783111501611-004

couldn't we be wrong in all cases? The solution to this problem, or better, the antidote to this confusion, lies in the reflection of the fact that any human practice, including the act of doubting, becomes meaningful only against the background of a larger web of practices, in which it is embedded. Any utterance of doubt, in order to be meaningful, must be brought forward within a context that itself is exempted from doubt. Or, as the 20th century philosopher Ludwig Wittgenstein puts it: "The game of doubting itself presupposes certainty."[4] Hence, there is no such thing as "being wrong in all cases." To counter al-Ghazālī's (and Descartes') thought experiment then, one could ask: Is al-Ghazālī's belief that he has put forward the claim "all my waking beliefs could in reality be imagined, unfounded and ineffectual" real, meaningful, and truth-apt, then that belief cannot be imagined, and turn out to be unfounded and ineffectual; hence, his claim is refuted. On the other hand, in case his belief is imagined, and turns out to be unfounded and ineffectual, then he has not made a claim that we could engage with in the first place. Al-Ghazālī, insofar as he is the subject of the act of claiming, inhabits a real world, in which it is possible to meaningfully speak and claim something; and from there, he looks at his other self that – insofar as it is the object of his claim – may be no more than a dream fantasy.[5]

The article at hand is not about radical scepticism and its futility.[6] Rather, the reason I brought up the dream argument is that it stems from the same sources that have fuelled a multitude of confusions about the nature and role of religious language and practice that have long pervaded and still do pervade analytic philosophy of religion. The growing discomfort with the way theology is done in analytic traditions has led to a call for "religion without metaphysics" or an abandonment of the "God of the philosophers" in favour of the "God of Abraham." To this end, the thought of Ludwig Wittgenstein has become a significant source of inspiration. This is not because the subject of religion looms large in his writings, which it does not, but because his radical critique of mainstream philosophy and his alternative can easily be extended to the field of religion. In fact, his way of doing philosophy does itself have a religious outlook, which may explain in part his quite enigmatic

---

4 Wittgenstein, Ludwig, *On Certainty*, ed. G.E.M. Anscombe/G.H. von Wright, transl. D. Paul/G.E.M. Anscombe, Oxford: Blackwell, 1997 [1st amended edition], §115.

5 This split of personality occurs, of course, to everyone who considers the dream argument meaningful, even if he or she does not assent to it. Thus, the argument should be considered meaningless.

6 For the dream argument in particular, see Stroll, Avrum, "Wittgenstein and the Dream Hypothesis," *Philosophia* 37, no. 4 (2009), 681–690. For a broader treatment of the incoherence of radical skepticism, see Schönbaumsfeld, Genia, *The Illusion of Doubt*, Oxford: Oxford University Press, 2016.

statement that he made to his friend Maurice Drury: "I am not a religious man, but I can't help see every problem from a religious point of view."[7] And, when Wittgenstein told his friend that his religious thought is not Greek, but a "hundred percent Hebraic,"[8] we can see him expressing a similar discomfort with the "God of the philosophers" that plagues a growing number of people in the study of religion. The article dovetails with this development and assumes that the opposites between the "God of the philosophers" and the "God of Abraham" – seen as labels for different approaches to religion – runs deep throughout the Islamic tradition.

The purpose of this study is threefold: First, I will elaborate on what is meant by the approach labelled as "God of the philosophers" and point to some of the confusions in religion that come along with it, especially with regard to the question of what it means that God is good. Secondly, I will outline the character of a Theology as Grammar, and then, thirdly, apply it to that particular question. The article will end with some final remarks. No pretence is made that this article represents a comprehensive treatment of the issues described; rather it should be understood as a preliminary investigation that will hopefully be followed by more profound monograph-length studies.

2 What are (Some of) the Problems?

In what follows, I will confine myself to two problem areas that are interconnected: First, I will discuss the development of the modern concept of "religion" and how this concept fortifies a problematic analytic philosophical approach to religion. Then, I will address several characteristics of how the word 'God' is understood within this approach and show that they are predicated on a confused understanding of religious language and practice.

2.1 The Modern Conception of Religion

There is a general agreement among researchers of religion that the genealogy of the modern notion of religion is closely tied to circumstances specific to (Western) European history and that the notion is therefore inappropriate and ill-suited to

---

7 For further elaborations on this statement, see Fronda, Earl S. B., *Wittgenstein's (Misunderstood) Religious Thought*, Leiden/Boston: Brill, 2010, 5ff.
8 Drury, Maurice, "Conversations with Wittgenstein," in: Rush Rhees (ed.), *Recollections of Wittgenstein*, 97–171, Oxford: Oxford University Press, 1984, 161.

both non-European traditions as well as pre-modern European Christianity. The Arabic term that is, at least since the end of the seventeenth century, most often translated as religion is *dīn*.[9] Its relative proximity to the modern European concept of
religion has been noted several times.[10] While also the modern notion is not unified
in itself, rather, it is understood with different accentuations depending on the context, one can safely establish four dominant usages of the word "religion":

a) *Religion as a generic singular*: To use "religion" as a generic singular (*Kollektivsin-
gular*) is problematic for several reasons. It invites one to believe that there is some
permanent and unchanging essence that is shared by anything that falls under the
term. Every statement, however, that begins with "Religion is . . ." either constitutes
a hollow generality or is simply wrong. Furthermore, what are held to be universal
features of religion are framed in terms of a historically contingent version of (Protestant) Christianity that serves as point of reference for defining and categorizing
non-Christian religious traditions.[11] Christianity is, in Friedrich Schleiermacher's
words, the "religion of the religions,"[12] the most complete manifestation of the concept of religion of which all other forms are deficient approximations and therefore

---

9 For an historical overview over how the word *dīn* has been rendered in Latin translations of the
Qur'ān, see Glei, Reinhold/Stefan Reichmuth, "Religion Between Last Judgement, Law and Faith:
Koranic *Dīn* and Its Rendering in Latin Translations of the Koran," *Religion* 42, no. 2 (2012), 247–271.
10 See Smith, Wilfred C., *The Meaning and End of Religion*, Minneapolis, Minn.: Fortress Press,
1991, chapter „The Special Case of Islam;" and more recently Abbasi, Rushain, "Islam and the Invention of Religion: A Study of Medieval Muslim Discourses on *Dīn*," *Studia Islamica* 116, no. 1
(2021), 1–106.
11 See Asad, Talal, *Genealogies of Religion: Discipline and Reasons of Power in Christianity and
Islam*, Baltimore/London: Johns Hopkins University Press, 1993, 42; Alatas, Syed F., *Religion and
Concept Formation: Transcending Eurocentrism*, London/New York: Routledge, 2016; Schulze,
Reinhard, *Der Koran und die Genealogie des Islam*, Basel: Schwabe Verlag, 2015, 161ff.; Ahmed,
Shahab, *What Is Islam? The Importance of Being Islamic*, Princeton, Oxford: Princeton University
Press, 2016, esp. 184–189.
  A recently published volume on Protestant notions of religion in Germany between the years
of 1830 and 1914 illustrates very well that though there is no and has never been a unified concept of religion in Protestant Christianity, one can nevertheless identify certain recurring elements that – in the course of Western colonialism – has shaped and still shapes dominant
globalized views on religion; see Pfleiderer, Georg/Harald Matern, (eds.), *Die Religion der Bürger:
Der Religionsbegriff in der Protestantischen Theologie vom Vormärz bis zum Ersten Weltkrieg*, Tübingen: Mohr Siebeck, 2021.
12 Schleiermacher, Friedrich, *Über die Religion*, Berlin: Reimer, [4]1831, 297. See also Dierken, Jörg,
"Transcendental Theories of Religion: Then and Now," in: Brent W. Sockness/Wilhelm Gräb
(eds.), *Schleiermacher, the Study of Religion, and the Future of Theology: A Transatlantic Dialogue*,
151–164, Berlin: De Gruyter, 2010, 159, and Pannenberg, Wolfhart, *Systematic Theology*, vol 1, ed.
Geoffrey Bromiley, London: Continuum International Publishing, 2004, 129–130.

rightfully object to Christian mission. Islam had an exceptional position due to its relatively close relationship to Christianity, as Ernst Troeltsch, another influential Protestant thinker, saw it. According to him, this would make evangelization of the Muslim lands hopeless, unless its ground is prepared through "weapons and colonization."[13] The devastating effects of a globalized hegemonic European modernity is visible up until today. From among them is the uprooting of Islamic tradition from its indigenous epistemic and conceptual heritage, which led to a (self-)alienation of the colonized from their past.[14]

In view of the problematic history of the word "religion" as a collective term but also because of its analytic inadequacy, some researchers have advocated for its complete abandonment in the field of Religious Studies or argued to treat "religion" as a family resemblance term.[15]

b) *Religion as a reified object*: The term "religion" as a reified concept suggests that there are several different religions,[16] each one of which can be objectified and put in comparison to the respective others. In the context of the development of an Enlightened natural religion of reason, but also in the context of European colonialism, this made it possible to adjudicate the truth-value of their respective doctrinal content from a supposedly neutral sphere of rationality, and it also gave rise to the construction of the so-called "World Religions."[17] This seems parallel to speaking of religion as a delimited domain that can be contrasted with other fields of human life that have been located outside the circle of religion, such as science and the

---

13 Troeltsch, Ernst, "Die Mission in der modernen Welt," in: Ernst Troeltsch (ed.), *Gesammelte Schriften, Zweiter Band: Zur Religiösen Lage, Religionsphilosophie Und Ethik*, 779–804, Tübingen: Mohr Siebeck, 1913 (repr. from Christliche Welt, 1906), 801. See also Schulze, *Der Koran und die Genealogie des Islam*, 506.

14 This can be seen among both Islamist and Modernist reformers; see, for example, Bauer, Thomas, *A Culture of Ambiguity: An Alternative History of Islam*, New York: Columbia University Press, 2021; Hallaq, Wael B., *The Impossible State: Islam, Politics, and Modernity's Moral Predicament*, New York: Columbia University Press, 2014; and Dabashi, Hamid, *Brown Skin, White Masks*, London: Pluto, 2011.

15 See for example Andrejč, Gorazd/Daniel Weiss (eds.), *Interpreting Interreligious Relations with Wittgenstein*, Boston: Brill, 2019, index s.v. "family resemblance;" and the concluding chapter in Abbasi, "Islam and the Invention of Religion;" Ahmed argues, though, in my opinion, not convincingly, against this approach, see Ahmed, *What is Islam?*, 240–243.

16 Peter Harrison even considers the emergence of a generic conception as a precondition for the possibility to speak about religions in the plural, see Harrison, Peter, *The Territories of Science and Religion*, Chicago/London: The University of Chicago Press, 2015, 101.

17 See Harrison, *Territories*, 102ff.; Masuzawa, Tomoko, *The Invention of World Religions: or, How European Universalism Was Preserved in the Language of Pluralism*, Chicago: University of Chicago Press, ³2007; and Schlieter, Jens, *Was ist Religion? Texte von Cicero bis Luhmann*, Stuttgart: Reclam, 2010, 13.

secular. Alleged neutral modes of secular reasoning denote the frame of reference, in which a comparison between these domains and the domain of religion takes place (e.g. "Religion and Politics," "Religion and Science," "Religion and Morality," and so on).

c) *Religion as an inward experience or sentiment*: A momentous shift happened in the European context when religion was no longer considered primarily a mode of worshipping God (*modus colendi Deum*) and a subordinate virtue of the cardinal virtue "justice," but as an inward experience or sentiment.[18] This inward experience was considered to be of universal character, and the core of revealed religion that otherwise is shaped by historical contingency. Immanuel Kant, for example, equated this core with pure Natural Religion *(Vernunftreligion)* in his work "Religion within the limits of mere reason;" while Friedrich Schleiermacher identified it with the "sense and taste of the Infinite."[19]

d) *Religion as a Set of Propositions (Doctrines) that Aims at Explaining the World and at Inducing Certain Inward and Outward Behaviour (Intentions, Moral Behaviour, Observance of Rituals and Commandments)*:
There is a close connection between the personalization of belief in Protestant thought and the conceptualization of religion as a set of propositions.[20] The latter can already be observed in the seventeenth century, in which "for a number of influential English Protestant thinkers (. . .), faith and belief were to be reduced to a cognitive act rather than a relational virtue. What made faith valid was the inherent rationality of the propositions toward which it was directed."[21] A century later, many Christian apologists as well as their foes, such as David Hume, while being radically antagonistic on many issues, nevertheless agree on the view that religion can effectively be reduced to a set of coherent propositions, while faith is nothing else than assent to their truth.[22] This notion of religion has been dominant ever since. However, it meets increasing opposition. By way of example, this is what Hent de Vries, professor of Religious Studies, writes on the issue:

---

18 See the summary of Ernst Feil's four volume study that traces the meaning of religion from early Christianity to 19th century Europe: Feil, Ernst, *Religio: Die Geschichte eines neuzeitlichen Grundbegriffs im 18. und frühen 19. Jahrhundert*, Göttingen: Vandenhoeck & Ruprecht, 2007, 879.
19 Feil, Ernst, "'Religio' and 'Religion' in the 18th Century: The Contrasting Views of Wolff and Edelmann," in: Jan Platvoet/Arie L. Molendijk (eds.), *The Pragmatics of Defining Religion: Contexts, Concepts and Contests*, 125–148, Leiden/Boston: Brill, 1999, esp. 142.
20 See Warner, Michael, "Is Liberalism a Religion?" in: Hent de Vries (ed.), *Religion: Beyond a Concept*, 610–617, New York: Fordham University Press, 2008, 612.
21 Harrison, *Territories*, 107.
22 Baird, Robert, "How Religion Became Scientific," in: Arie L. Molendijk/Peter Pels (eds.), *Religion in the Making: The Emergence of the Sciences of Religion*, 205–231, Leiden, Boston: Brill, 1998, 218.

So much is clear: beyond the modern definition of the concept, which has so often, and all too hastily, identified "religion" with a "set of beliefs" – in any case, with a mental state or series of states of consciousness, whose content and mode could be described by propositions that map ideas onto the world (albeit an ideal or mythically past and future one) – an altogether different sense or set of senses of the term ought to be envisioned.[23]

The idea that religion is first and foremost a set of propositions suggests believing that the meaning and truth of these propositions could be ascertained independently from religious practice. In this case, religious practice amounts to a likely, though not necessary consequence of holding a certain set of religious propositions true. This is equally problematic, as we will see later, since the idea of meaning and truth of propositions (be they religious or not) as something that is logically independent from human practices is a confused one.

Although there is no necessary relationship between these four dominant understandings of the modern concept of religion, they are historically intertwined. "Religion" is fully domesticated within the modern secular project's normative conceptual terrain that defines the modern ordering of reality and rationality – not least by generating a set of binaries such as *"belief* and *knowledge, reason* and *imagination, history* and *fiction, symbol* and *allegory, natural* and *supernatural,* [and] *sacred* and *profane."*[24] A critical reflection from an outside perspective of modern life has become very difficult, as, to speak with Charles Hirschkind, the "secular is the water we swim in."[25] This may explain in part why many friends and foes of religion have unthinkingly embraced the secular notion that the most proximate place to truth and the highest forms of rationality manifest in the language and methods of natural (or empirical) sciences. They only differ on where to place religion in this epistemic framework. The foes consider religion to be either a primitive form of natural sciences (e.g. Auguste Comte's Law of the Three Stages), or a theoretical explanation of the world that has been at war with science ever since,[26] or a bunch of unfalsifiable and, therefore, meaningless propositions.[27] On the other hand,

---

23 Vries, Hent de, "Introduction: Why Still 'Religion'?" in: Hent de Vries (ed.), *Religion. Beyond a Concept,* 1–98, New York: Fordham University Press, 2008, 5.

24 Asad, Talal, *Formations of the Secular: Christianity, Islam, Modernity,* Stanford: Stanford University Press, 2003, quote from p. 23 (emphasis in the original).

25 Hirschkind, Charles, "Is There a Secular Body?" *Cultural Anthropology* 26, no. 4 (2011), 634.

26 Suleiman, Farid, "Ist Islamische Theologie eine Wissenschaft?" in: Abbas Poya/Farid Suleiman/Benjamin Weineck (eds.), *Bildungskulturen im Islam: Islamische Theologie Lehren und Lernen,* 43–72, Berlin/Boston: De Gruyter, 2022, 46–53 (for further literature, see there, fn. 16).

27 Exemplified in Antony Flew's paper "Theology and Falsification" (1950) of only three and a half pages length that stirred much debate; reprinted in Flew, Antony, "Theology and Falsification," in: Antony Flew/Alasdair MacIntyre (eds.), *New Essays in Philosophical Theology,* 96–99, London: SCM Press, 1963 [1955]. I will get back to this paper below.

friends of religion have argued that the truth of (a particular) religion can be assessed in a way very similar to the methods of science. The outcome is a certain type of philosophical theism that is, as Ingolf Dalferth rightly put it, a "rational artificial product of modern natural religion" (*rationales Kunstprodukt neuzeitlicher Vernunftreligion*).[28] Even though the heyday of this kind of theism might have been in the 19th century – when one of its most famous representatives, William Paley, published his widely received work "Natural Theology" in 1802, and others, such as the quite unconventional figure Charles Voysey (d. 1912) pushed Natural Theology to further extremes – theism remains a vital force with significant influence, especially in the field of analytic philosophy of religion. Vivid examples of different sorts of philosophical theism can be seen in theologians such as Alvin Plantinga, William Lane Craig and Richard Swinburne. The latter, for example, uses Bayes's theorem to measure the truth probability of what he calls theological hypotheses such as "God exists" or "Jesus was resurrected from the dead." According to Swinburne, the former is more likely to be true than untrue (>50%) while the latter can be established with a probability of 97%.[29]

It is this view of religion as a set of scientific hypotheses that aims at providing a theoretical explanatory model of God, world, and history that a growing number of theologians of different affiliation, including the author of the article at hand, consider to be a philosophical confusion and grave misapprehension of what revealed religion (in this case, Islam) is about. The modern notion of religion has become so dominant and globalized that one has to reflect upon it regardless of what religious tradition one wants to study, in order to avoid painting a distorted picture of that tradition. Furthermore, although the modern notion of religion constitutes a radical break from those that came before, there are remarkable similarities to be found in Muslim tradition (maybe with the exception of point (c) above). See, for example, what the famous 12th-century theologian Fakhr ad-Dīn ar-Rāzī has to say about how to recognize true religion (*ad-dīn al-ḥaqq*):

> There is no way of discerning true religion except by theoretical investigation (*naẓar*). Theoretical investigation does not mean anything else than the structuring of premises in order to derive conclusions. If premises as such would always be inferential, then they would all be in need of further (more basic) premises, which amounts to either circular reasoning or

---

28 Dalferth, Ingolf U., *Die Wirklichkeit des Möglichen: Hermeneutische Religionsphilosophie*, Tübingen: Mohr Siebeck, 2003, 257.

29 See Swinburne, Richard, *The Existence of God*, Oxford: Clarendon Press, 2004, and Swinburne, Richard, "The Probability of the Resurrection," in: Andrew Dole/Andrew Chignell (eds.), *God and the Ethics of Belief: New Essays in Philosophy of Religion*, 117–130, Cambridge: Cambridge University Press, 2005.

an infinite regress. Both is invalid, hence, inferential premises must finally go back to necessary knowledge (*ḍarūriyyāt*).[30]

For ar-Rāzī, true religion, then, is a kind of philosophy that can be spelled out in
terms that come close to what is called evidentialist and foundationalist. Contrary
to modern notions of philosophy, ar-Rāzī does view practice such as performing
rituals and following certain commandments an integral part of his philosophy –
and in this much his philosophical *dīn* is best understood as what Pierre Hadot
called *manière de vivre* – however, he reduces the practical dimension to the instrumental role of predisposing the intellect to the acquisition of knowledge.[31] It
is of little surprise, then, that for ar-Rāzī as for many others in the tradition of
falsafa and *kalām*, religious doctrines not only have propositional character, but
their meaning is also thought to be logically independent from practice.

Part of the explanation why many modern readers of the Classical age of
Muslim tradition particularly sympathize with the works of *falsafa* and *kalām*
(esp. the Muʿtazilite version of the latter) is that they are able to relate more
closely to the concept of reason and religion advocated in these traditions. Furthermore, the proofs for God's existence worked out by Muslim philosophers like
Ibn Sīnā (Avicenna, d. 1037/428) and *kalām* theologians like al-Ghazālī remain a
vital source for theism, as can be seen, for example, in the work of the above-
mentioned Christian apologist William Lane Craig.[32]

The God of theism is often labelled as the "God of the philosophers," at whom
we look more closely in the following.

2.2 The God of the Philosophers

In a broad sense, the term "God of the philosophers" does not merely signify a certain notion of God, but encompasses a whole range of different, yet internally related (pre)suppositions. These (pre)suppositions, though they took various forms
and accentuations over the course of history, can essentially be traced back to
Plato. The God of the philosophers is not only at the heart of the metaphysical tradition found in *falsafa*, but also significantly shaped *kalām* theology. The same is true

---

30 Rāzī, Fakhr ad-Dīn, ar-, *at-Tafsīr al-Kabīr aw Mafātīḥ al-Ghayb*, 32 vols., Cairo: Maktabat al-
Kulliyyāt al-Azhariyya, 1934–64, 6:13.
31 Janos, Damien, "Intuition, Intellection, and Mystical Knowledge: Delineating Fakhr Al-Dīn Al-
Rāzī's Cognitive Theories," in: Frank Griffel (ed.), *Islam and Rationality: The Impact of Al-Ghazālī.
Papers Collected on His 900^(th) Anniversary*, vol. 2, 189–228, Leiden/Boston: Brill, 2016, 207, 208, 212,
213 and 218.
32 See Craig, William L., *The Kalām Cosmological Argument*, Eugene, Or.: Wipf and Stock, 2000.

with regard to Western thought up until Hegel; and it was this very same God that Nietzsche declared dead a few decades later.[33] As has been the subject of numerous publications written by the learned pen of Georg Picht, it was the modern notion of the autonomous subject that deposed the God of the philosophers from his throne, leaving some of his characteristics intact, while throwing others away. Since the details of this development are beyond the scope of this paper, it will suffice to quote a passage of Picht's work that condenses some of the major aspects of the issue:

> The so called "God of the philosophers" manifests itself in the form of cognition that we nowadays call "theory." The obviousness of axiomatic reasoning, the absolute validity of the law of non-contradiction, the concept of "substance," the theory of categories and the hegemony of logic cannot be explained until one has grasped that in this very basic structure of European thought an appearance of the divine takes place, which origin we can trace back to Greek mythology in all its essential developmental stages.[34]

The God of the philosophers, I would add, is particularly alive in the realm of analytic philosophy of religion, and the modern notion of religion discussed above is, in part, one of its offshoots.

In what follows, I will briefly summarize some of the integral interrelated components of the God of the philosophers that will render visible contours of its manifestation in the Islamic tradition (the most important parts of the following sentences are highlighted in italics):

God's thought is the source of the *immutable rational structure of reality*. By means of the rational soul, which is itself of divine nature, *human beings can partake in the thoughts of God*, looking thereby at reality from His perspective. Knowledge about the structure of reality is theoretical and expressed in *logic (middle terms of syllogisms), definitions, and abstract rational principles*, which nonetheless are *more aptly placed in the realm of ontology than epistemology*, as they describe primarily fundamental features of reality and only secondarily those of human cognition. The more the soul is prepared to connect with the divine to acquire theoretical knowledge, the more *likeness to God* is attained. Herein lies the *primary goal of philosophy*, which, however, is impossible to realize in full.[35] The main obstacle consists in the

---

33 Since Nietzsche considered Christianity a kind of Platonism, he did not differentiate between the Christian God and that of the philosophers.

34 Picht, Georg, "Einleitung," in: Georg Picht/Rudolph Enno (eds.), *Theologie – Was Ist Das?*, 9–47, Stuttgart/Berlin: Kreuz, 1977, 14 (my translation).

35 Platon speaks of *homoíosis theō katà tò dynatón*, see Theaitetos, 176. Accordingly, in the Islamic tradition philosophy was defined as *at-tashbīh bi-llāh bi-ḥasab aṭ-ṭāqa al-insāniyya*, see Hein, Christel, *Definition und Einteilung der Philosophie: Von der spätantiken Einleitungsliteratur zur arabischen Enzyklopädie*, Frankfurt am Main: Lang, 1985, 118f.

material "prison" of the soul, that is the human body.[36] Against the background of this *sharp distinction between body and soul, religious practice is given a mere instrumental role* in the sense that it facilitates the preparedness of the soul to acquire theoretical knowledge.[37] While, in principle, anyone can achieve relative likeness to God, in reality, only very few people actually do so. They constitute a small philosophical elite that must sharply be distinguished from the rest of humanity, who, due to their poor rational abilities, *should not be confronted with philosophical ideas* in the first place. The uneducated masses, however, do have a distinctive role and place within the just order of the polity as imagined by the philosophers, and in order to integrate fully therein, *they have to be tamed.* This is done through the means of *religion – a poor copy of philosophical truth* palatable to those uninitiated to philosophy. Against this backdrop, it does not come as a surprise that *a prophet is nothing else than a philosopher* who is able to *translate philosophical truth into allegorical and metaphorical language*, as is found, for example, in the Qur'ān.[38]

Incidentally, I would argue that categorizing intellectual traditions in Islamic history based on how near they draw to the God of the philosophers will prove more meaningful than categorizations such as rationalist vs. traditionalist or those based on whether their respective method rests on presuppositions or not.[39] *Falsafa* would then be a tradition in which the God of the philosophers is manifested in the most obvious way, but still in *kalām* theology – especially from the time after al-Ghazālī – this God is all too present. To name but a few parallels: In *kalām*, the structure of reality (including God) is considered to be in line with logic and supposedly necessary principles; that makes it possible to discuss God as a theoretical object of inquiry, determining thereby what is necessary, possible or impossible with regard to God's essence and His attributes. Also, *kalām* has, over the course of the centuries, taken over much of the noetic framework found

---

36 Ibn Sīnā states: "As long as the rational soul is associated with the human body, no corporeal entity [jirm] can be completely ready to receive the divine effluence or have perfectly revealed to it all the intelligibles." See his *Risāla fī l-kalām fī n-nafs an-nāṭiqa*, translated in Gutas, Dimitri, *Avicenna and the Aristotelian Tradition: Introduction to Reading Avicenna's Philosophical Works*, Leiden/Boston: Brill, [2]2014, 73.

37 See, for example, fn. 30 above.

38 For further details, see Griffel, Frank, "Muslim Philosophers' Rationalist Explanation of Muhammad's Prophecy," in: Jonathan E. Brockopp (ed.), *The Cambridge Companion to Muhammad*, 158–179, Cambridge: Cambridge University Press, 2010.

39 For example, Ulrich Rudolph argues that „theological speculation – even that of the Muʿtazila – was never truly free from presuppositions" and should therefore not be considered to fall under the broad term "philosophy." See Rudolph, Ulrich, "Introduction," in: Ulrich Rudolph (ed.), *Philosophy in the Islamic World: Volume 1: 8th–10th Centuries*, 1–28, Leiden/Boston: Brill, 2017, 18–21; quote from 20.

in *falsafa*, with the effect of naturalizing prophecy and stressing the instrumental role of practice. Finally, the sharp distinction between the elite and commoners is familiar to every student of *kalām*.

I want to conclude this subchapter with two brief examples of which the first touches on the question, whether God exists, and the second on the question, whether God is good. This will help to further elucidate the philosophical concept of God.

2.2.1 Does God Exist?

The issue of proving the existence of a creator (*wujūd aṣ-ṣāniʾ*) was of central concern to Islamic philosophers and theologians throughout the centuries.[40] Up until today, it is a widespread opinion among theists and atheists alike that the sentence "God exists" has meaning independently from any human practice and forms a hypothesis that can be subject to rational inquiry. As I will argue later, both are untenable, but for now, I am concerned with the issue that most *kalām* theologians take it for granted that the Qurʾān entails their theology. A case in point is the Qurʾānic story of Abraham trying to convince his people to abandon false gods such as the moon, the stars and the sun and to turn to their creator, *Allah*.[41] Without going into too much detail, the *kalām* theologians took what Abraham had to say about the moon, the stars and the sun to essentially boil down to the philosophical argument that anything that is subject to change is temporal, while anything that is temporal belongs to the category of possible existence.[42] God, in contrast, is eternal and exists necessarily.[43] According to *kalām* theologians, the Qurʾān addresses many other philosophical problems such as the

---

[40] The proofs put forward by them have commonly been interpreted as proofs for God's existence. Quite recently, Hannah Erlwein argued that Classical Islamic theologians and philosophers did not intend or seek to prove that God exists – since they took his existence for granted – but first and foremost aimed at establishing God's attribute as being the creator. See Erlwein, Hannah, *Arguments for God's Existence in Classical Islamic Thought*, Berlin/Boston: De Gruyter, 2019. I found her claim thought provoking but not convincing enough. Discussing her study would, however, go beyond the scope of this paper.

[41] See Qurʾān 6:74–83.

[42] This philosophical conviction can be traced back to Greek philosophy. In Latin Europe up until the modern age, it was formulated, inter alia, as "nullum mutabile est necessarium hinc omne mutabile est contingens."

[43] For further information on how the story was interpreted by *kalām* theologians with a focus on Fakhr ad-Dīn ar-Rāzī, see Oulddali, Ahmed, *Raison et révélation en Islam: Les voies de la connaissance dans le commentaire coranique de Faḫr al-Dīn al-Rāzī*, Leiden/Boston: Brill, 2019, 228f.

issue of human free will and (but to a far lesser extent) that of theodicy. Abū al-Ḥasan al-Ashʿarī (d. 936/324), the eponym of the Ashʿarite school of *kalām*, extended this, in some way, to the prophetic tradition, when he argued that the reason why the Prophet Muhammad did not speak about intricate issues of theology such as the question of the createdness of the Qurʾān was not that he wasn't familiar with these (as indeed, according to al-Ashʿarī, he was), but that, in his time, there was no need to raise them.[44] The narrative that the Qurʾān (or the Islamic revelation in general) anticipates later *kalām* theology is still present and vivid; it even shines through in M.A.S. Abdel Haleem's contribution to the *Cambridge Companion to Classical Islamic Theology*. There, he gives a summary account of Qurʾānic theology that comes unexpectedly close to the methods and teachings that evolved a few centuries later within (esp. Ashʿarite) *kalām*. Reading the Muslim scripture in that way, it seems only logical to conclude, as Abdel Haleem does, that the Qurʾān "provides an original model for dialectical theology."[45]

I completely disagree with this assessment. The Qurʾān is not a philosophical book, nor does it share the metaphysical presuppositions upon which the traditions of *falsafa* and *kalām* rest. The God of the philosophers is approached by the questions "What is He?" and "How does He relate to the world ontologically?," while the God of the Qurʾān, in contrast, is presented through questions such as "Who is He?" and "How does He relate to creation 'ethically'?"[46] The Qurʾān is neither a forerunner of dialectical theology, nor does it make sense to the Qurʾān, as I will elaborate further later on, to take God as a theoretical object whose existence, like that of any other "thing," can be subject to inquiry.

In what follows, I am going to contrast two different interpretations of two Qurʾānic verses, found at 52:35–36, that constitute obvious candidates for an alleged Qurʾānic proof of God's existence. The first interpretation is that of the contemporary thinker Muhammad Asad (d. 1992), whom I have taken here merely as

---

44 Suleiman, Farid, *Ibn Taymiyya und die Attribute Gottes*, Berlin/Boston: De Gruyter, 2019, 86, fn. 430.

45 Abdel Haleem, M.A.S., "Qur'an and Hadith," in: Tim Winter (ed.), *The Cambridge Companion to Classical Islamic Theology*, 19–32, Cambridge: Cambridge University Press, 2008, 26 and 31. No less perplexing, but somehow understandable if read in light of the above, is Abdel Haleem's claim that early *kalām* "originated completely in the Islamic environment and foreign elements came only later as a result of mixing with other nations and also as a result of translating Greek texts into Arabic." Abdel Haleem, M.A.S., "Early Kalām," in: Seyyed H. Nasr/Oliver Leaman (eds.), *History of Islamic Philosophy*, 71–88, London/New York: Routledge, 1996, 79.

46 What I called "ethically" for lack of an alternative expression could be misunderstood as relating to ethics as a subfield of philosophy that engages in a systematic inquiry into the moral principles of human conduct. The actual meaning that I intended here will become clear in the course of this paper.

a representative of the many exegetes who read the Qur'ān through the lenses of philosophy. It is found in his annotated English translation of the Qur'ān. I will juxtapose this with the interpretation put forward by the famous exegete Abū Ja'far Ibn Jarīr aṭ-Ṭabarī (d. 923/310), whose exegetical work of the Qur'ān remains largely unaffected by *falsafa* and *kalām*. The difficulty, initially, is that a neutral rendering of the verses in English does not seem possible, so I will first cite the Arabic original and then go directly into Asad's treatment of them.

أم خلقوا من غير شيء أم هم الخالقون [Q 52:35] أم خلقوا السموات والأرض بل لا يوقنون [Q 52:36]

This is translated and annotated by Muhammad Asad as follows:

> (52:35) [Or do they deny the existence of God?[20]] Have they themselves been created without anything [that might have caused their creation]?[21]-or were they, perchance, their own creators?
> (52:36) [And] have they created the heavens and the earth?[22] Nay, but they have no certainty of anything!
> *Note 20:* I.e., implicitly, by denying the fact of His revelation.
> *Note 21:* I.e., by "spontaneous generation," as it were.
> *Note 22:* This is a *reductio ad absurdum* of their unwillingness to admit the existence of a conscious Primary Cause underlying all creation.[47]

Asad adds the whole clause „Or do they deny the existence of God?," and comments in a footnote – seemingly aware of the fact that the initial hearers of the Quran did not doubt the existence of God in the first place – that anyone who denies the Quranic revelation implicitly denies God's existence. While I have difficulties seeing why this should be the case, what is more important here is that Asad's translation makes it obvious that he understands the two verses to form a cosmological argument for the existence of God, or, in Asad's words, for the existence of a conscious Primary cause.

This stands in stark contrast to aṭ-Ṭabarī's interpretation, who, even though he is famous for listing all sorts of different kinds of interpretations in his exegetical work, does not even consider the possibility that the two verses speak about God's existence. Here is what he writes pertaining to these two verses:

> God [rhetorically] asks the polytheists, whether they have not been created from/through (*min*) fathers and mothers, so that they are like lifeless stones [with respect to not having

47 Asad, Muhammad, *The Message of the Qur'ān: The Full Account of the Revealed Arabic Text Accompanied by Parallel Transliteration*, Bristol: Book Foundation, 2008. All brackets, footnote symbols and italics in the original; to distinguish the footnotes, I added *"Note 20:"* and so on.

been created through anything] that neither comprehend or grasp any of God's argument, nor ponder any [of the Qur'ānic] lessons, nor are admonished by any [of the Qur'ānic] harangues (. . .).

God's [rhetorical] question [of the subsequent verse] "are they the creators?" means: Are they the creators of creation so that they do not obey God's commandments, and they do not abstain from what He has prohibited, since it is the creator who is entitled to issue commands and prohibitions? (. . .)[48]

To illuminate this further, I will paraphrase the two verses in a way that fits with aṭ-Ṭabarī's understanding of them: "Are the polytheists like inanimate entities that would be excused from being unable to grasp the Qur'ānic message? Or do they believe to have created themselves, the heavens and the earth so that they think God has no right to call for their obedience?"

I would argue that for aṭ-Ṭabarī, as for large parts of the Islamic tradition, the question whether God exists barely makes sense. This is not, because they have an irrational or fideist approach to religion, but because the question itself rests on metaphysical assumptions that this tradition, and I would argue, also the Qur'ān, does not share.

2.2.2 Is God Good?

In this subchapter, I want to juxtapose two thinkers who could seemingly not be more different when it comes to their respective intellectual background. The first is Antony Flew, a staunch atheist of immense influence. He has been quite often (but wrongly) associated with logical positivism, because he seriously questioned the meaningfulness of theological assertions in his famous paper "Theology and Falsification" presented in 1950.[49] The other one is the already mentioned Fakhr ad-Dīn ar-Rāzī, a committed Muslim and one of the most famous representatives of 12th-century *kalām*. What makes a comparison between the two worthwhile is that they reach, as we will see in the following, surprisingly similar conclusions when it comes to the question of whether God is good. The reason for that is that the God whose existence Flew denies is the same one that ar-Rāzī affirms, namely, the God of the philosophers.

---

48 Ṭabarī, Ibn Jarīr, aṭ-, *Tafsīr aṭ-Ṭabarī. Jāmiʿ al-Bayān ʿan Taʾwīl Ay Al-Qurʾān*, ed. ʿAbd Allāh aṭ-Turkī, 30 vols., Cairo: Dār Hajr, 2001, 21:596.
49 Flew turned to Deism eight years before his death in 2010, which is, however, not relevant for the discussion at hand. For his paper, see fn. 26 above.

As has been said, Flew raises grave doubts about the meaningfulness or intelligibility of a whole range of things that religious believers say about God. To illustrate this, let us take the utterance "God is good" as an example. Flew argues that since for the believer nothing counts as falsification of this utterance, it has no positive content either. He writes:

> For if the utterance is indeed an assertion, it will necessarily be equivalent to a denial of the negation of that assertion. And anything which would count against the assertion, or which would induce the speaker to withdraw it and to admit that it had been mistaken, must be part of (or the whole of) the meaning of the negation of that assertion. And to know the meaning of the negation of an assertion, is as near as makes no matter, to know the meaning of that assertion. And if there is nothing which a putative assertion denies then there is nothing which it asserts either: and so it is not really an assertion.[50]

So, for example, religious people assert that God loves human beings like a father. But isn't it the case, Flew asks, that earthly fathers make every effort to protect their children, while so many people die from diseases without the intervention of the heavenly father? Religious believers, then, qualify the statement above saying that God's love is not like human love. The problem with that is that anytime anything occurs that goes against the seemingly positive content of utterances such as "God is good" or "God loves His creation," the utterance is further qualified, until it dies, as Flew puts it, "the death by a thousand qualifications."[51]

We find quite the same position, in ar-Rāzī's writings, yet from a theist perspective. There, he argues that if we apply human rational standards of morality to God, it turns out that His acts are neither wise nor benevolent. Since it is indisputable, however, that God is in fact wise and benevolent, the meaning of wisdom and benevolence is, when it comes to God, unintelligible. Hence, human reason cannot provide any meaningful criteria for what the sentence "God is good" means; any attempt to do so, leads, in the long run, to the conclusion that God is, in fact, evil. For example, we say that a queen is benevolent when she compensates the good deeds that her servants have done for her in a generous manner. In contrast, she would be just if she punishes when her servants have purposefully harmed her for no valid reason. God is, as ar-Rāzī argues, not like the human queen, since He is not in need of anyone's deeds nor can He be harmed by anyone; moreover, whatever He gives as reward does not minder what He has and involves no efforts on His part. God, however, imposes a burdensome system of commandments, knowing that many will disobey Him. He rewards a few and destines many to hell, while He Himself was neither benefitted nor harmed; and

---

50 Flew, "Theology and Falsification," 98.
51 Flew, "Theology and Falsification," 96f., quote from 97.

while He could easily have created all humans for paradise. While the human queen mentioned above is indeed wise, benevolent and just, God's actions appear to be arbitrary, or even foolish and evil. Ar-Rāzī goes on for pages to list further examples of a similar kind, showing thereby the futility of trying to grasp God's wisdom and goodness in human terms. I will finish with one additional example: Being benevolent to someone requires that this someone is in need of what he receives. Giving a cure to someone who is sane or giving money to the rich is, therefore, no act of charity. Since God, however, is the source of all things, be they bad or good, He Himself caused the state that His charitable act responds to. Therefore, He is like a doctor who wounds someone and then cures him, or like a queen who takes money from someone and then makes him rich again. Once more, reason declares the doctor and the queen as evil and foolish, and if reason were allowed to be extended to God's actions, it would necessarily come to no other conclusion.[52]

Even though the context of discussion is a totally different one, ar-Rāzīs chapter could be read also as a vivid demonstration that any attempt for theodicy is a hopeless task. What is more important here, is that the (former) atheist Antony Flew and the theist ar-Rāzī derive in a very similar way the conclusion that theological assertions such as "God is good" are unintelligible.

3 "Theology as Grammar" as a Therapy for Philosophical Confusions

3.1 The Character of a "Theology as Grammar"

In the course of unfolding what a Theology as Grammar may amount to, the following three quotations from Wittgenstein's *works* provide a good starting point:[53]

---

52 Rāzī, Fakhr ad-Dīn, ar-, *al-Maṭālib al-'āliya*, ed. Aḥmad as-Saqqā, 9 vols, Beirut: Dār al-Kitāb al-'Arabī, 1987, 3:289ff. (for example, 291f. and 299ff.).
53 In a strict sense, only the *Tractatus logico-philosophicus* counts as a work of Wittgenstein, because he did not only intend it for publication, but also did so within his lifetime. In a broader sense, also the *Philosophical Investigations* and less so his *On Certainty* can be considered works of Wittgenstein. This is not the case with the posthumously published notes taken either by himself or by his students during his lectures, which nevertheless constitute a further important source for investigating into Wittgenstein's thought.

[1] Practice gives the words their sense.[54]
[2] How words are understood is not told by words alone (theology).[55]
[3] Grammar tells what kind of object anything is (Theology as grammar).[56]

All three statements constitute interrelated cornerstones of Wittgenstein's general view on language and two of them make explicit reference to theology. This is not because Wittgenstein was a theologian or particularly interested in theology (both of which he wasn't), rather, it is more likely that he believed that prevalent misunderstandings about the character of language are especially prevalent in certain kinds of theology. One of these misunderstandings forms much of the background against which to read the three quotes above. It is what Wittgenstein calls the Augustinian picture of language. Wittgenstein describes it as follows: "Every word has a meaning. This meaning is correlated with the word. It is the object for which the word stands."[57] To illustrate this by an example, if someone says "There is a chair in the room next to us," the word chair stands for a particular object that is identical with its meaning. This view implies that words in and by themselves have meaning in virtue of their relation to their respective referent. From here, it is easy to see how the idea of a context-independent meaning could have developed. This meaning is described as the real meaning or the essence of the word, which implies that the more context is needed in identifying a word's meaning, the farther away that actual meaning is diverted from that essence (or what is more commonly called "literal meaning"). In search for that essence, one, probably a philosopher, has to take "a view from nowhere," which means that one has to abstract from any context-dependent or ordinary use of the word.

For Wittgenstein, this understanding of language and meaning is not only in itself confused, but also gave rise to further confusions that have long pervaded and still do pervade the field of philosophy and theology. In his opinion, many words do actually not refer to objects, and even if they do, it is not the object that constitutes the word's meaning. If someone asks about the meaning of the word "chair," for example, one may very well answer by pointing to a chair. This is not because the chair itself is the meaning of the word, but rather because this is one of many ways to teach someone how the word "chair" is used. The word "chair," like any other, plays a certain role in our language, inextricably linked to human practices in which it finds its application. A very common meaning of the word "meaning," though not the only one, is identical with the use of a certain word; and taken in this sense, the meaning of the word "chair" is its use. The use is gov-

---

54 CV, 85e.
55 Zettel, section 144.
56 PI §373; see also Wittgenstein's Lectures, 320f.
57 PI §1.

erned by an open-ended and variable set of rules – and this is what Wittgenstein calls grammar. Hence, an investigation into the grammar of the word "chair" is likewise an investigation into the word's meaning.

Let us look at a different word, namely "consciousness," and try to relate it to what has been said so far. The word "consciousness" plays different roles in different contexts, and we all are familiar with its grammar in the sense that we know how to use and understand the word. So, for example, we know what it means to say that someone lost consciousness in an accident and we likewise know what it means to say that someone lost a chair. Furthermore, we know that it makes sense to say to the one who lost his chair that it must still be somewhere around or that we try to help him searching for it, while it does not make any sense to say or do the same with regard to someone who lost consciousness. So, the grammar of the word "chair" and that of the word "consciousness" is similar in some respects, but different in others. One of the main sources of confusion in philosophy and theology lies in ignoring the differences in grammar or at least not taking them sufficiently into account, and the issue of "consciousness" is a prime example of that. This is due to the assumption that there is a word-world-relationship that can be investigated as such or independently from how the word is used in a certain context. In fact, it is here, where the meaning that is of philosophical interest is to be found; all others are, in contrast, merely contingent on the context in which the word is used. From a philosophical viewpoint, then, the relevant question is not what it means when someone says about a patient that she lost or regained consciousness, rather one has to isolate the word "consciousness" from all possible contexts and then inquire into its meaning. That is, however, an impossible task, since there is no context-independent meaning in the first place. Therefore, what the philosopher in fact does is unthinkingly transfer the word "consciousness" from its original home in language to the home that words like "chair" inhabit. This is, because everyday language about objects like chairs seems so natural that one easily overlooks that it is, as any other way of talking, embedded in a certain context and practice that makes it meaningful. Hence, philosophical talk about consciousness neither takes place in the abstract nor is context-independent, rather it is aligned to the way one talks about empirical objects such as chairs. Consciousness, then, becomes some delimitable object in our imagination, an immaterial entity of mysterious nature that the philosopher has to investigate by asking questions like: What is consciousness or what does it consist of? How is it connected to the body? Is it identical with the self and if not, how is it related to it?

Since the meaning of the word "consciousness" is, in this philosophical view, fixed by its referent, it seems that we do not really know the word's meaning unless we are able to answer these questions. It must, then, appear strange that people know perfectly well how to use the word "consciousness" (or more often, "conscious") in daily life and that they are generally easily understood, while the question "What is consciousness?" seems nebulous. Here, one is reminded of Augustine's famous remark that he knew what time is provided that nobody asks him.[58]

For Wittgenstein, words like "consciousness," "time," and one could add, "truth" and "reality," are not more surrounded by an aura of dark mystery than are words like "chair," "tree" and "cat." All these words do not mean something by virtue of an assumed word-world relationship that can be investigated in the alleged abstract, but by virtue of their application in practice. To know what each word means, is to know how it is used. This is not true only with regard to these words, but also with any other, including the one that concerns us most here, the word "God."

Philosophy and theology are, in its dominant forms, concerned with problems that would not have arisen in the first place if the differences in grammar would have been carefully considered. But even though we are competent in using words, we are unable to view the complexities of grammar from a bird's eye view. Hence, Wittgenstein writes: "A main source of our failure to understand is that we do not survey the use of our words. – Our grammar is lacking in this sort of surveyability."[59] Grammar in that sense is not a delimited clear set of rules, and this is why its investigation will always remain partial and limited to a particular question or problem. That exactly is what a *Theology as Grammar* would amount to. And in that sense, Theology as Grammar does not purport to put forward a new theory about God and creation, neither does it solve any of the intricate theological problems that existing theories pretend to clear up. This is not, because these problems are too difficult or that we lack sufficient information in order to solve them, but because they are in themselves confused in the sense that they only arise, as Wittgenstein says, "when language goes on holiday."[60] Hence, Theology as Grammar is to be understood as a therapy that is applied in concrete cases of philosophical confusion caused by the "bewitchment of our intelligence through the means of language."[61] And I would argue, ar-Rāzī (and no less Flew) fell victim to language's bewitchment; and this brings us to the next chapter, in which we will see an example of how a Theology as Grammar may be applied.

---

58 Augustine, *Confessiones*, Book XI, Chapter XIV. See also Wittgenstein's discussion of Augustine in the Blue Book: Wittgenstein, Ludwig, *The Blue and Brown Books: Preliminary Studies for the "Philosophical Investigations,"* Oxford: Blackwell, [2]1969, [reprint, 2007], 26.
59 Wittgenstein, *Philosophical Investigations*, §122.
60 Wittgenstein, *Philosophical Investigations*, §38.
61 Wittgenstein, *Philosophical Investigations*, §133 and 109.

3.2 God's Goodness in Light of a "Theology as Grammar"

3.2.1 The Language Trap or Why ar-Rāzī's Notion of God's Goodness is a Confused One

The first major step towards philosophical confusion is to disregard the complex and diverse application that words find in practice, and to try and find the one and only valid yardstick by which one may determine the essential meaning of a word, and subsequently, the truth of a proposition containing that word. This yardstick is taken from a context that is so common that we unthinkingly believe it to be a natural given, though in reality, it is no less contingent on that particular context than any other yardstick would be on its respective context. The context I speak of is the one of daily interaction with other human beings.[62] Once this step is taken, it is not so important whether philosophers agree on how exactly to define this yardstick. With regard to the word "good," we may think of the following yardstick:

> To say that "xyz" is good is to say that the good consequences of his or her deeds morally justify the bad consequences or, in case they don't, it was not in xyz's power to prevent the bad consequences from happening.

Xyz stands for any person or person-like being, be it Zayd, Peter, whoever happens to be ar-Rāzī's neighbour, or, and that is most relevant here, God. Based on that, philosophers may come to one of the following conclusions:

a) God is good, because He created the best of all possible worlds. In other words, all evil that we see in our world is logically necessary and therefore God cannot be blamed for it (This is a widespread theist notion).

b) God is either nonexistent or a monster, because our world is full of evil that could easily have been prevented; or, as some say, our world seems to be the worst of all possible worlds (Whoever holds such a view would probably identify as an atheist).

c) Applying the yardstick reveals that the sentence "God is good" is false. The yardstick is, as such, correct and reason cannot come up with an alternative one, nevertheless, we know beyond any doubt that God is good. Hence, it must be that human reason is incapable of explaining what it means that God is good (That is ar-Rāzī's position).

---

62 In which, of course, there are many possible yardsticks and not one that is necessary.

Since all three views start from the seemingly innocuous assumption that the meaning of the sentence "God is good" and the sentence "ar-Rāzī's neighbour is good" can be assessed by one and the same yardstick, it follows that all three also share the following: God is, like ar-Rāzī's neighbour, a possible part of one's life; hence, whether God is good or not is contingent upon His behaviour. Therefore, in order to have faith (īmān) in God's goodness one has to analyse what God does (and the three views above are the outcome of such analysis).

The views mentioned above seem – even if unconsciously – to imagine God as a metaphysical, immaterial superhuman who combines together all positive human traits in the most perfect manner. In that sense, God is not only considered some external object that the theist, in contrary to the atheist, believes to exist beside all other real objects, but also the goodness of God and that of ar-Rāzī's neighbour is considered only different in degree, not in substance. Let us contrast this with another trait of God, namely, that He is beautiful, as we are informed by a narration that is attributed to the Prophet Muhammad.[63] Certainly, the word beautiful is not reserved for God alone, rather we might also describe, for example, the Alps or Mona Lisa as beautiful. While it would be awkward, if not nonsensical, to compare the beauty of the Alps with the beauty of Mona Lisa, one might very well condemn it as blasphemous to include God in that comparison. Had God, however, not been imagined as an immaterial superhuman, but as a corporeal one, it would be no surprise if one would find corresponding comparisons in the books of philosophy or theology.

Such considerations, but also the fact that ar-Rāzī finally cannot help but to render God's goodness meaningless in the end, and the fact that Antony Flew notes with full astonishment that believers describe God as good regardless of what happens within their life, shows that there is something inherently wrong with applying one and the same yardstick to statements such as "God is good" and "ar-Rāzī's neighbour is good." This will be further explored in the upcoming subsection, when we look at a non-confused understanding of God's goodness.

---

63 The whole narration reads as follows: "The Prophet, peace and blessings of Allah be upon him, said: 'No one will enter Paradise who has an atom's-weight of pride in his heart.' A man said, 'What if one likes his clothes to look good and his shoes to look good?' He said, 'Allah is beautiful and loves beauty. Pride means denying the truth and looking down on people.'" Muslim, Ṣaḥīḥ Muslim, 2 vols., Vaduz: Thesaurus Islamicus Foundation, 2000, narration nr. 275.

3.2.2 A Non-Confused Understanding of God's Goodness

Let us begin by imagining two people sitting in a desert, gazing up at a star-filled sky during a clear night. Both are deeply moved by this overwhelming experience, but in totally different ways. The first person is awestruck by the beauty and the harmony manifested in the sky, seeing in each and every luminous dot above a sign that points to the majesty and glory of its creator. A profound feeling of love and veneration seeps into every fibre of that person's being; a feeling that he seeks to exhibit, knowing that words cannot express the praise that this creator deserves. He falls on his knees in the sand, prostrates himself and addresses his creator from the bottom of his heart by saying "Glory and praise be to *Allah*, as many times as the number of his creatures and creation, as much as pleases Him, as heavy in the scale as His throne, and as infinite as the ink required to record his words."[64]

The other person is no less touched by the dazzling starry sky, but as I said, in a totally different way. He is struck by the vastness of the dark sky with its countless shining lights in a manner that induces in him a deep and profound feeling of the arbitrariness, randomness and purposelessness of existence as a whole. He feels somehow humbled by the fact that he, like anything else, is no more than an insignificant product of blind forces, acting in accordance with immutable and aimless natural laws. At the same time, he finds himself helplessly exposed to these blind forces – an insight that comes along with a profound feeling of anxiety. In addition to that, a deep sense of freedom arises in him, insofar as he realizes that no other than he himself bears the burden to define what it means to be a human being.

Surely, the two described reactions upon contemplating the starry night sky are by no means exhaustive. What is more important, however, is the fact that the difference of reactions is located on a different level than a disagreement about, for example, how far away from earth a particular object in the starry sky is. The difference between the two levels is not one of degree, but of kind. The following, interrelated points will illustrate this claim:

First, we have a deep feeling that even if all possible questions of science are settled unanimously, the existential questions of life have still not been touched at all.[65] This in contrast to questions like that regarding the distance between planet earth and other objects in space.

---

64 A common prayer found in the Islamic tradition; see, for example, Muslim, *Ṣaḥīḥ Muslim*, narration nr. 7088.
65 As noted by Wittgenstein in his *Tractatus Logico-Philosophicus*, ed. C. K. Ogden, Hoboken: Taylor and Francis, 2014 [1922], 6.52.

Secondly, and that dovetails with the first point, let's imagine two people talking about the distance between the sun and the earth. The one says that it is about 150 million kilometres, to which the other responds that this may very well be true. We would conclude that the two opinions expressed are quite close to each other. If they, however, discuss in the same way the question of whether there is a God who created us all, we would, in contrast, infer that there is an enormous gulf between these two persons.[66]

Thirdly, let us look at how the Qur'ān speaks about the rejection of the many signs (ayāt) that God has put into creation and revelation, of which each one points to different elements that undergird an Islamic way of life, and that find its most concise expression in the phrase lā ilāha illā Allāh (there is nothing worthy of worship except Allāh).[67] Those who reject these signs are repeatedly described as being covered in darkness, deaf, dumb and blind, having hearts that are affected by disease or even sealed by God, and God has led them astray. The signs in creation and revelation are recognizable only for those, as the Qur'ān teaches us, who, for example, "do believe (yu'minūn)," "are certain (yūqinūn)," "understand (ya'qilūn)," "take heed (yadhdhakkarūn)," "are God-fearing (yattaqūn)," "know (ya'lamūn)," and "are steadfast and thankful (ṣabbār shakūr)."[68] There, we see a profound connection between religious knowledge and ethics; not knowing God and, hence, being ignorant of His signs is, as opposed to not knowing the distance between sun and earth, an ethical failure, not a mere cognitive incapacity.[69]

All three points indicate that neither īmān nor kufr is contingent upon knowledge of certain "facts" in the world, and in that sense, they are also not to be equated with rival theories about the world.[70] The believer and the unbeliever may inhabit the same "world of facts," and they may agree on the same scientific theories that try to explain this world, nevertheless, the former lives in a world of creation and the latter in one governed by blind nature. In that sense, īmān and kufr are better understood as different ways of seeing and living one's life. Īmān, then, encompasses several regulative pictures such as God, creation, revelation, afterlife, responsibility, that find meaningful application in the life of the believer.

---

66 The same thought with different examples can be found in Wittgenstein, Ludwig, *Culture and Value*, ed. G. H. von Wright, Oxford: Blackwell, 1977, 53.

67 Commonly translated as "There is no god except *Allah*" and boiled down to an affirmation of the existence of a particular being called *Allah*. This reading is alien to the context of revelation and must be seen in light of later philosophical discourses. It impoverishes, and I would add, misconstrues the actual meaning of that Quranic phrase.

68 Q 6:99, 2:118, 2:164, 6:126, 10:6, 6:97, 14:5.

69 By this, I do not intend to say that knowing the distance between sun and earth is not likewise embedded in human practice, such as, for example, the practice of mathematics.

70 This is not to say that facts are, in contrast, objectively accessible in a positivist sense.

In order to investigate the meaning of each picture one has to look at how they are applied within the life of the believer. Also, the pictures might increase in intensity, but it also might very well happen that they fade. Some of the possible means in order to restore their force consist of reading the Qur'ān, praying, fasting, or doing other types of good deeds, visiting graves in order to remember death, pondering the miraculous nature of creation, but also going through certain experiences in life such as illnesses or other types of suffering. All this presupposes that the pictures have not faded away completely, or, in other words, that the pictures still find at least some application in life. Recognizing the signs of God in creation and revelation, then, is itself a manifestation of *īmān*, fear of God, and of thankfulness and patience as the above cited verses indicate. The unbeliever may agree with the believer on each and every scientific theory regarding the world, but again, the latter sees the divine names manifested everywhere, while for the former, nothing of this kind finds any meaningful application in life. And in case it starts to do so, it is not because the unbeliever double-checked the facts, but because the whole way of looking at them has changed. Transition from belief to unbelief or vice versa, then, is of such a profound and radical nature that it is rightfully described as conversion.

The Qur'ān is a repository of all the relevant religious pictures that account for Islamic belief or *īmān*. The Qur'ān teaches us the meaning of these pictures by showing us how they are embedded and applied in the life of the prophets. It is here where we find the meaning of these pictures, and the more we grasp it (which entails living by it), the more our lives approximate to that of the prophets. Hence, understanding the Qur'ānic descriptions of God does not manifest in some theoretical knowledge about a certain type of being, but in an Islamic way of life. It is then no surprise to see that the Qur'ānic descriptions all fit two characteristics: They are directly related to creation and they find meaningful application in worship (in a broad sense of worship that can be equated with an Islamic way of life). For example, God is the creator, while we are created; God is first and last, while we all are ephemeral; God is mighty and knowing, while we are weak and ignorant; God is the Provider and Guide, while we are in need of provision and guidance; God is forgiving and merciful, while we are sinful and in need of mercy; and so on. The Qur'ān provides a normative framework of how to relate meaningfully between creator and creation in religious practice. Having internalized these rules, either consciously or unconsciously, and applying them correctly in practice makes one a competent participant of the Islamic (or Prophetic) way of life. In other words, the Qur'ān is like a textbook of religious grammar, it provides the believer with regulative pictures and examples of prophets who are masters when it comes to the application of these pictures in life.[71]

Contrast this with philosophical descriptions that turn God into an object of theoretical study, such as God being pure existence, free of substance and accidents, eternal, non-spatial, non-temporal, and so on. By this, the philosophers transfer the picture "God" from its original home in prophetic practice to the practice of dispassionate scientific or theoretical investigation. If the approach of a "Theology as Grammar" is correct, much of the intellectual tradition of *falsafa* and *kalām* turns out to be based on a gross misunderstanding of the character of religious language. For example, all the ontological problems about God – so prominent in Muslim theology – that were inferred from the fact that the Qur'ān describes God as speaking, would then not constitute deep and complicated issues that only the scholarly elite has insight into.[72] Rather, it would be more aptly compared to the response of a little child who has not yet learned the correct use of the word "consciousness," and therefore says, after hearing that one of his relatives lost consciousness, that he will set out on a search for it.[73]

After this quite lengthy, but necessary introduction, we finally get to the question of how a "Theology as Grammar" would look at a sentence such as "God is good." For that purpose, we look at two other sentences, namely, "All human beings are sinners" and "My neighbour is a criminal." I will use the grammar of "sinner" and "criminal" to highlight the differences between the respective grammar of the word "good" as understood by a "Theology as Grammar" and a philosophical theology. Even though both words (i.e., sinner and criminal) share in the notion of delinquency, I believe that the difference between their grammars are more obvious than the differences between the grammars of the word "good" applied as attrib-

---

71 As the positivist understanding of "facts" is untenable, so is the view that the Qur'ān is meaningful in and through itself. Rather, reading and interpreting the Quran are practices that shape and are shaped by the larger web of practices, in which they are embedded.
72 Against the background of Aristotelian ontology and the assumed rational principle that anything that is subject to change is temporal (see fn. 41 above), the question arose how God can meaningfully be described as having addressed time-bound human beings (such as the prophets Moses, Jesus and Muhammad) with a human language (such as Hebrew, Aramaic and Arabic). Over the course of the centuries, Muslim theologians worked out different theories of remarkable sophistication to solve the problem.
73 Or, in the words of Wittgenstein: "When we do philosophy, we are like savages, primitive people, who hear the way in which civilized people talk, put a false interpretation on it, and then draw the oddest conclusions from this." Wittgenstein, *Philosophical Investigations*, §194. However harsh this remark may sound, one has to bear in mind that Wittgenstein intentionally picks up a dominant self-conception of philosophy, which sharply distinguishes between the intellectual elite and the ignorant masses, and then turns it against philosophy itself.

utes to God and ar-Rāzī's neighbour. Seeing these differences will help to clarify an adequate understanding of the different roles of the word "good."

As has become clear, philosophical theology treats the statement "God is good" like a proposition such as "My neighbour is a criminal." The truth value of both statements is contingent upon certain "facts" in the world. It is nothing that I can initially know, rather I have to check the facts and as long as I haven't, there is no rational basis to conclude them as either true or false. In contrast, a "Theology as Grammar" would affirm the above with regard to the statement "My neighbour is a criminal." For example, if someone says "My neighbour is a criminal," it would make sense to respond with, for example, "No, he isn't, he's an innocent law-abiding citizen" or "What makes you so sure, have you seen him breaking the law?" and so on. Any analogous conversation with regard to the statement "God is good" would, in contrast, hardly be meaningful. This needs further clarification. Let us look at the sentence "All human beings are sinners," a statement that is attributed to the prophet Muhammad.[74] This statement is not to be understood as the outcome of an empirical study on whether there has been a single human being who completely abided by God's commandments. Rather, being a sinner and, hence, being in constant need of God's forgiveness is not contingent upon certain behaviour. It is a deep and profound attitude that runs through every fibre of the believer's being; or in other words, it is a regulative picture that finds its application in an Islamic way of life, and is not contingent on certain events that happen in that life. Our worship of God is deficient, neither do our words express the praise He deserves nor do we remember Him sufficiently in our lives. That we do not give full right to God's glory in our worship is, however, a core element in the Muslim's relationship with God; it is not a question of finding more adequate words to praise God or to increase the activity of remembering God. It is nonsense to say that, for example, if you use these words or if you remember God a billion times (or any other number) in your life, then you have given due rights to the glory of God in your worship. This is further supported by a narration, according to which the prophet Muhammad has taught his disciples that none, not even he or any other prophet, will enter paradise by his or her deeds alone, but only by God's mercy. Again, this should not be understood in the sense that it is theoretically possible to acquire enough good deeds to fully deserve paradise, but it just so happens that human beings are unable to acquire them. Rather, it means that we human beings are inherently sinful and perma-

---

74 The full saying reads: "All human beings are sinners. And the best of the sinners are those that permanently seek God's forgiveness." See Tirmidhī, Abū 'Īsā, at-, *Sunan at-Tirmidhī*, Vaduz: Thesaurus Islamicus Foundation, 2000, hadith nr. 2687. Also in the Qur'ān, the prophets repeatedly pray for God's forgiveness and mercy.

nently in need of God's forgiveness, regardless of our behaviour. Hence, to say that one is not in need of God's forgiveness would itself be a blameworthy and sinful statement even in the highly unlikely event that one has never gone against any of God's commandments. Saying such a thing would indicate that one has not yet grasped the profound nature of the relationship between the creator and the human being that is at the heart of Islamic ethics. In contrast, claims such as "My neighbour is a criminal" have indeed to be checked against contingent facts in our world in order to determine their truth value. In that sense, this statement describes something that happens in one's life. Statements such as "God is good," then, are more similar in grammar to statements such as "All human beings are sinners" than to statements such as "My neighbour is a criminal;" the former are not about contingent facts that the believer comes across after checking the state of the world, rather they express a regulative picture that is part of a larger web of pictures pertaining to an Islamic way of life. In that sense, God is not, like the neighbour, in the believer's life, rather the believer's life is in God.

4 Final Remarks

I want to end my paper with three remarks. The first one reiterates points that have been already mentioned, but are of central importance for adequately understanding the character of a "Theology as Grammar." The other two concern follow-up questions that I have not raised; not because they are less significant, but for reasons of space.

One has to keep in mind that regulative pictures are not to be understood as being logically prior to practice in the sense that the picture in itself contains its meaning. Rather, in order to know what the picture means, one has to look at how it is used, or to use another term, to investigate its grammar. This is not something specific to religious language, but is likewise true in ordinary speech about cats, dogs, tables and chairs. For the Muslim believer, the Qur'ān is the most important textbook of religious grammar, teaching him or her how to use words like "God" and His many names in an Islamically meaningful way. That does not mean that one consciously acquires all the rules of correct application, rather it is comparable to a child's learning the language of his or her parents, which also happens without learning concrete syntactical or grammatical rules. When Wittgenstein says in the *Blue Book* that "we don't use language according to strict rules – it hasn't been taught us by means of strict rules, either,"[75] he

---

75 Wittgenstein, *The Blue and Brown Books*, 25.

wants to dispel the idea that grammar is some sort of fixed algorithm that we mechanically apply when we speak. Hence, any general remark about the uses of a word – or what Wittgenstein calls "grammatical remarks" – neither expresses a (metaphysical) necessity, nor an autonomous calculus, and not even a theoretical insight about language and meaning. Also, they are no less context-dependent than any other type of remark would be. Hence, a "Theology as Grammar" is applied in concrete cases, for example, where we are trapped by the similarities of grammars and overlook the much more profound differences between them. In such a case, we treat as the same what should, in fact, be treated differently. We then may derive philosophical or theological problems that are discussed for centuries in the hope that someday we will find the right answer. This is where a "Theology as Grammar" has to step in, reminding us of the differences of the grammars at work. The desired outcome of that is to see that the problems actually cannot be solved, but only dissolved, because they are based on confusions about language. In that sense, "Theology as Grammar" is, as I said above, like a therapy that finds application in specific situations.

Secondly, a Wittgensteinian approach to Theology is at risk of being faced with different charges, especially that of anti-realism, fideism and relativism. The scope of the paper did not allow to discuss these charges, nevertheless I deem it inappropriate to end this article without at least saying a few words on the topic. Wittgenstein's thought does not call for adapting and reshaping some elements of the framework within which dominant forms of philosophy and theology operate, rather it demands a paradigm shift that necessitates the breaking down of the framework as a whole. Binaries such as anti-realism, fideism, relativism and their respective counterparts such as metaphysical foundationalism are outcomes of this framework, or, to use a phrasing by Hilary Putnam, "manifestations of the same disease."[76] A disease that Wittgenstein wanted to treat with his philosophy of language. It is regretful, though comprehensible that many interpretations of Wittgenstein dismiss the radical outlook of his thought and try to domesticate it within the dominant environment of philosophy. It is, then, no big surprise that charges against Wittgenstein such as the ones listed above are repeated over and over again in much of the secondary literature.[77]

---

76 Putnam, Hilary, *Renewing Philosophy*, Cambridge, MA: Harvard University Press, 1992, 177.
77 On the other hand, there are many who try to correct this distorted picture of Wittgenstein. I will suffice with the following selection: Taylor, Charles, "Overcoming Epistemology," in: Charles Taylor (ed.), *Philosophical Arguments*, 1–19, Cambridge, MA/London: Harvard University Press, [2]1995, and Phillips, D. Z., "Wittgensteinianism: Logic, Reality, and God," in: William J. Wainwright (ed.), *The Oxford Handbook of Philosophy of Religion*, 447–471, New York/Oxford: Oxford University Press, 2007.

Thirdly, my Wittgensteinian approach to understanding of the Islamic sources – the Qur'ān and the Prophetic tradition – raises the question of how much Wittgenstein is contained in the Islamic tradition. I would say that there is much to find if one does not fathom the Islamic tradition, as is commonly done, through lenses tinted by notions of religion prevalent in modernity and the God of the philosophers – both of which I have problematized above. Especially interesting in this regard is the prominent Damascene theologian Ibn Taymiyya (d. 1328), to whom I have dedicated much of my research in the past years.[78] The similarity of his thought to that of Wittgenstein has been repeatedly noted in the literature (though most of the time only in passing). Ibn Taymiyya has not only put forward a profound critique of philosophical and theological thought that boiled down Islam to questions of ontology, but also worked out an alternative vision of it that has ethics at its core.[79] Admittedly, some of his own views were to a considerable extent affected by the very philosophical discourse he criticised, however, through my reading of Wittgenstein I came to understand more fully how deep-rooted the rejection of the God of the philosophers is in Ibn Taymiyya's thought. This definitely deserves to be explored more fully, and I have noticed with delight that no less an authority on the topic of religion than Talal Asad, himself a reader of Wittgenstein for many decades, has come to somewhat similar conclusions.[80]

Bibliography

Abbasi, Rushain, "Islam and the Invention of Religion: A Study of Medieval Muslim Discourses on *Dīn*," *Studia Islamica* 116, no. 1 (2021), 1–106.

Abdel Haleem, M.A.S., "Early Kalām," in: Seyyed H. Nasr/Oliver Leaman (eds.), *History of Islamic Philosophy*, 71–88, London/New York: Routledge, 1996.

Abdel Haleem, M.A.S., "Qur'an and Hadith," in: Tim Winter (ed.), *The Cambridge Companion to Classical Islamic Theology*, 19–32, Cambridge: Cambridge University Press, 2008.

Ahmed, Shahab, *What Is Islam? The Importance of Being Islamic*, Princeton, Oxford: Princeton University Press, 2016.

Alatas, Syed F., *Religion and Concept Formation: Transcending Eurocentrism*, London/New York: Routledge, 2016.

Andrejč, Gorazd/Daniel Weiss (eds.), *Interpreting Interreligious Relations with Wittgenstein*, Boston: Brill, 2019.

---

[78] See Suleiman, *Ibn Taymiyya und die Attribute Gottes*. An English translation of this book recently appeared at Brill: Suleiman, Farid, Ibn Taymiyya and the Attributes of God, trans. Carl Sharif El-Tobgui, Leiden/Boston: Brill, 2024.

[79] See, for example, Hoover, Jon, *Ibn Taymiyya*, London: Oneworld, 2019, 42ff.

[80] See Asad, Talal, "Thinking About Religion Through Wittgenstein," *Critical Times* 3, no. 3 (2020), 403–442.

Asad, Muhammad, *The Message of the Qur'ān: The Full Account of the Revealed Arabic Text Accompanied by Parallel Transliteration*, Bristol: Book Foundation, 2008.

Asad, Talal, *Genealogies of Religion: Discipline and Reasons of Power in Christianity and Islam*, Baltimore/London: Johns Hopkins University Press, 1993.

Asad, Talal, *Formations of the Secular: Christianity, Islam, Modernity*, Stanford: Stanford University Press, 2003.

Asad, Talal, "Thinking About Religion Through Wittgenstein," *Critical Times* 3, no. 3 (2020), 403–442.

Baird, Robert, "How Religion Became Scientific," in: Arie L. Molendijk/Peter Pels (eds.), *Religion in the Making: The Emergence of the Sciences of Religion*, 205–231, Leiden/Boston: Brill, 1998.

Bauer, Thomas, *A Culture of Ambiguity: An Alternative History of Islam*, New York: Columbia University Press, 2021.

Craig, William L., *The Kalām Cosmological Argument*, Eugene, Or.: Wipf and Stock, 2000.

Dabashi, Hamid, *Brown Skin, White Masks*, London: Pluto, 2011.

Dalferth, Ingolf U, *Die Wirklichkeit des Möglichen: Hermeneutische Religionsphilosophie*, Tübingen: Mohr Siebeck, 2003.

Descartes, René, *Oeuvres De Descartes. Nouvelle Présentation*, ed. Charles Adam/Paul Tannery, 11 vols, Paris: J. Vrin, 1982–91.

Dierken, Jörg, "Transcendental Theories of Religion: Then and Now," in: Brent W. Sockness/Wilhelm Gräb (eds.), *Schleiermacher, the Study of Religion, and the Future of Theology: A Transatlantic Dialogue*, 151–164, Berlin: De Gruyter, 2010.

Drury, Maurice, "Conversations with Wittgenstein," in: Rush Rhees (ed.), *Recollections of Wittgenstein*, 97–171, Oxford: Oxford University Press, 1984.

Erlwein, Hannah, *Arguments for God's Existence in Classical Islamic Thought*, Berlin/Boston: De Gruyter, 2019.

Feil, Ernst, "'Religio' and 'Religion' in the 18th Century: The Contrasting Views of Wolff and Edelmann," in: Jan Platvoet/Arie L. Molendijk (eds.), *The Pragmatics of Defining Religion: Contexts, Concepts and Contests*, 125–148. Leiden/Boston: Brill, 1999.

Feil, Ernst, *Religio: Die Geschichte eines neuzeitlichen Grundbegriffs im 18. und frühen 19. Jahrhundert*, Göttingen: Vandenhoeck & Ruprecht, 2007.

Flew, Antony, "Theology and Falsification," in: Antony Flew/Alasdair MacIntyre (eds.), *New Essays in Philosophical Theology*, 96–99, London: SCM Press, 1963 [1955].

Fronda, Earl S. B., *Wittgenstein's (Misunderstood) Religious Thought*, Leiden/Boston: Brill, 2010.

Glei, Reinhold/ Reichmuth, Stefan, "Religion Between Last Judgement, Law and Faith: Koranic *Dīn* and Its Rendering in Latin Translations of the Koran," *Religion* 42, no. 2 (2012), 247–271.

Griffel, Frank, "Muslim Philosophers' Rationalist Explanation of Muhammad's Prophecy," in: Jonathan E. Brockopp (ed.), *The Cambridge Companion to Muhammad*, 158–179, Cambridge: Cambridge University Press, 2010.

Gutas, Dimitri, *Avicenna and the Aristotelian Tradition: Introduction to Reading Avicenna's Philosophical Works*, Leiden/Boston: Brill, [2]2014.

Hallaq, Wael B., *The Impossible State: Islam, Politics, and Modernity's Moral Predicament*, New York: Columbia University Press, 2014.

Harrison, Peter, *The Territories of Science and Religion*, Chicago/London: The University of Chicago Press, 2015.

Hein, Christel, *Definition und Einteilung der Philosophie: Von der spätantiken Einleitungsliteratur zur arabischen Enzyklopädie*, Frankfurt am Main: Lang, 1985.

Hirschkind, Charles, "Is There a Secular Body?" *Cultural Anthropology* 26, no. 4 (2011), 633–647.

Hoover, Jon, *Ibn Taymiyya*, London: Oneworld, 2019.

Janos, Damien, "Intuition, Intellection, and Mystical Knowledge: Delineating Fakhr Al-Dīn Al-Rāzī's Cognitive Theories," in: Frank Griffel (ed.), *Islam and Rationality: The Impact of Al-Ghazālī. Papers Collected on His 900th Anniversary*, vol. 2, 189–228, Leiden/Boston: Brill, 2016.

López-Farjeat, Luis Xavier, "al-Ghazālī on Knowledge ('ilm) and Certainty (yaqīn) in al-Munqidh min aḍ-Ḍalāl and al-Qisṭās al-Mustaqīm," in: Georges Tamer (ed.), *Islam and Rationality: The Impact of Al-Ghazālī. Papers Collected on His 900th Anniversary*, vol. 1, 229–252, Leiden/Boston: Brill, 2015.

Masuzawa, Tomoko, *The Invention of World Religions: Or, How European Universalism Was Preserved in the Language of Pluralism*, Chicago: University of Chicago Press, 3'2007.

Muslim, *Ṣaḥīḥ Muslim*, 2 vols., Vaduz: Thesaurus Islamicus Foundation, 2000.

Oulddali, Ahmed, *Raison et révélation en Islam: Les voies de la connaissance dans le commentaire coranique de Faḫr al-Dīn al-Rāzī*, Leiden/Boston: Brill, 2019.

Pannenberg, Wolfhart, *Systematic Theology*, vol 1, ed. Geoffrey Bromiley, London: Continuum International Publishing, 2004.

Pfleiderer, Georg/Matern, Harald (eds.), *Die Religion der Bürger: Der Religionsbegriff in der Protestantischen Theologie vom Vormärz bis zum Ersten Weltkrieg*, Tübingen: Mohr Siebeck, 2021.

Phillips, D. Z., "Wittgensteinianism: Logic, Reality, and God," in: William J. Wainwright (ed.), *The Oxford Handbook of Philosophy of Religion*, 447–471, New York/Oxford: Oxford University Press, 2007.

Picht, Georg, "Einleitung," in: Georg Picht/Rudolph Enno (eds.), *Theologie – Was Ist Das?*, 9–47, Stuttgart/Berlin: Kreuz, 1977.

Putnam, Hilary, *Renewing Philosophy*, Cambridge, MA: Harvard University Press, 1992.

Rāzī, Fakhr ad-Dīn, ar-, *at-Tafsīr al-Kabīr aw Mafātīḥ al-Ghayb*, 32 vols., Cairo: Maktabat al-Kulliyyāt al-Azhariyya, 1934–64.

Rāzī, Fakhr ad-Dīn, ar-, *al-Maṭālib al-'āliya*, ed. Aḥmad al-Saqqā, 9 vols, Beirut: Dār al-Kitāb al-'Arabī, 1987.

Rudolph, Ulrich, "Introduction," in: Ulrich Rudolph (ed.), *Philosophy in the Islamic World: Volume 1: 8th–10th Centuries*, 1–28, Leiden/Boston: Brill, 2017.

Rudolph, Ulrich (ed.), *Philosophie in der islamischen Welt: 11. und 12. Jahrhundert: Zentrale und östliche Gebiete*, Basel: Schwabe Verlag, 2021.

Schleiermacher, Friedrich, *Über die Religion*, Berlin: Reimer, 4'1831.

Schlieter, Jens, *Was ist Religion? Texte von Cicero bis Luhmann*, Stuttgart: Reclam, 2010.

Schönbaumsfeld, Genia, *The Illusion of Doubt*, Oxford: Oxford University Press, 2016.

Schulze, Reinhard, *Der Koran und die Genealogie des Islam*, Basel: Schwabe Verlag, 2015.

Smith, Wilfred C., *The Meaning and End of Religion*, Minneapolis, Minn.: Fortress Press, 1991.

Stroll, Avrum, "Wittgenstein and the Dream Hypothesis," *Philosophia* 37, no. 4 (2009), 681–690.

Suleiman, Farid, *Ibn Taymiyya und die Attribute Gottes*, Berlin/Boston: De Gruyter, 2019.

Suleiman, Farid, "Ist Islamische Theologie eine Wissenschaft?" in: Abbas Poya/Farid Suleiman/ Benjamin Weineck (eds.), *Bildungskulturen im Islam: Islamische Theologie Lehren und Lernen*, 43–72, Berlin/Boston: De Gruyter, 2022.

Swinburne, Richard, *The Existence of God*, Oxford: Clarendon Press, 2004.

Swinburne, Richard, "The Probability of the Resurrection," in: Andrew Dole/Andrew Chignell (eds.), *God and the Ethics of Belief: New Essays in Philosophy of Religion*, 117–130, Cambridge: Cambridge University Press, 2005.

Ṭabarī, Ibn Jarīr, aṭ-, *Tafsīr aṭ-Ṭabarī. Jāmi' al-Bayān 'an Ta'wīl Ay Al-Qur'ān*, ed. 'Abd Allāh at-Turkī, 30 vols., Cairo: Dār Hajr, 2001.

Taylor, Charles, "Overcoming Epistemology," in: Charles Taylor (ed.), *Philosophical Arguments*, 1–19, Cambridge, MA/London: Harvard University Press, 2'1995.

Tirmidhī, Abū ʿĪsā, at-, *Sunan at-Tirmidhī*, Vaduz: Thesaurus Islamicus Foundation, 2000.
Troeltsch, Ernst, "Die Mission in der modernen Welt," in: Ernst Troeltsch (ed.), *Gesammelte Schriften, Zweiter Band: Zur Religiösen Lage, Religionsphilosophie Und Ethik*, 779–804, Tübingen: Mohr Siebeck, 1913 (repr. From Christliche Welt, 1906).
Vries, Hent de, "Introduction: Why Still 'Religion'?" in: Hent de Vries (ed.), *Religion. Beyond a Concept*, 1–98, New York: Fordham University Press, 2008.
Warner, Michael, "Is Liberalism a Religion?" in: Hent de Vries (ed.), *Religion: Beyond a Concept*, 610–617, New York: Fordham University Press, 2008.
Watt, William M., *The Faith and Practice of Al-Ghazālī*, London: George Allen and Unwin, 1953.
Wittgenstein, Ludwig, *The Blue and Brown Books: Preliminary Studies for the "Philosophical Investigations,"* Oxford: Blackwell, [2]1969, [reprint, 2007].
Wittgenstein, Ludwig, *Culture and Value*, ed. G. H. von Wright, Oxford: Blackwell, 1977.
Wittgenstein, Ludwig, *On Certainty*, ed. G.E.M. Anscombe/G.H. von Wright, transl. D. Paul/G.E.M. Anscombe, Oxford: Blackwell, 1997 [1st amended edition].
Wittgenstein, Ludwig, *Philosophical Investigations*, ed. G. E. M. Anscombe/Peter M. S. Hacker/Joachim Schulte, Chichester, West Sussex, U.K/Malden, MA: Wiley-Blackwell, [4]2010.
Wittgenstein, Ludwig, *Tractatus Logico-Philosophicus*, ed. C. K. Ogden, Hoboken: Taylor and Francis, 2014 [1922].

Suggestions for Further Reading

Mustafa, Abdul Rahman, "Ibn Taymiyyah & Wittgenstein on Language," *The Muslim World* 108, no. 3 (2018), 465–491.
Suleiman, Farid, "*Fiṭra*, Sünde und Zweifel im Koran. Eine sprachpragmatische Annäherung mit Wittgenstein," *Hikma* 12 (2021), 119–144.

Farid Suleiman, Daniel H. Weiss, Genia Schönbaumsfeld

Epilogue

The epilogue consists of three parts, written by the authors of the three chapters, discussing the contributions of the other two authors from their own perspective.

Part One

Farid Suleiman

My fellow authors have focused on issues that seemed peculiar to their respective religious tradition. The idea of God having a name, discussed by Daniel Weiss, is not a totally unfamiliar one in the Islamic tradition, according to which God has not only one but many names. Yet, there are significant differences. Among the many controversies around God's names in the Islamic tradition, such as on the question of whether God could rightfully be named "the Creator" *before* He created anything, there is, to the best of my knowledge, none that comes close to the specific issue that Daniel Weiss addressed in his article. Even more obvious is the case with the issue of the Trinity. Since the Qur'ān rejects the concept in its entirety, the Muslim tradition did not have to cope with the problems discussed by Genia Schönbaumsfeld. Even though there are many good reasons to engage with other religious traditions, one might have the suspicion here that the discussions within the Jewish and Christian traditions are of little relevance to Islamic theology in this case, due to the peculiarity of the topics. Such a conclusion would, however, be short-sighted and superficial.

While it is important to take the peculiarities of the intellectual traditions of Judaism, Christianity and Islam into account, they must not be allowed to obscure the structural similarities that exist between these traditions. These similarities partly arise from the fact that all three traditions have been under the influence of Greek thought, but also shaped each other over the centuries. Furthermore, with regard to more recent times, the rise and spreading of secularism and the new modes of knowledge production that came along with it challenged all three traditions in similar ways. From among these structural similarities is the recurrent manifestation of the struggle between "the God of the Philosophers" and "the God of Abraham" in the history of the three traditions. A more comprehensive description, inspired by Wittgenstein, that would allow to include other intellectual traditions as well, in fact, all human thought, is to say that this struggle is

https://doi.org/10.1515/9783111501611-005

about resisting the temptation to surrender to the all-levelling power of language instead of surrendering *to life*.[1]

There are plenty of examples in the Islamic tradition, I would argue, that prove that victory in this struggle is achievable. Regrettably, those inside and outside the Islamic tradition who have been less successful in this struggle have tried to domesticate such approaches to make them fit their preconceived notions of rationality. Alternatively, in cases where this seemed not viable, they have readily dismissed them as irrational, crude, naïve, fideistic, or the like. There are analogous developments in the Jewish and Christian tradition, and by exploring them, I hope to gain a more profound comprehension of the disputes within the Islamic tradition and to find inspiration for resolving them. Wittgenstein proves particularly helpful in explicating the sources and characteristics of this above-mentioned struggle. Conversely, religious, or more generally, non-philosophical traditions can provide us with valuable insights into Wittgenstein's ideas or enable us to refine and expand upon them as necessary. This is unsurprising, given that Wittgenstein himself described his thinking as Hebraic and juxtaposed it against the Greek tradition. Moreover, it is worth noting that non-philosophical traditions, such as that of Native Americans, did in fact have an impact on Wittgenstein's thought, albeit indirectly, by way of American pragmatism.[2]

Comparative studies on the intellectual history of Judaism, Christianity and Islam are numerous. However, they often focus on thinkers or philosophical systems that have been heavily influenced by Greek philosophy – Maimonides, Thomas Aquinas and Ibn Sīnā – are some examples of thinkers who are frequently drawn upon in research. This might be motivated by, among others, the hope that the common Greek philosophical background of their thought results to achieving greater comparability. Yet, comparative studies of traditions within these three religions that are not inclined to philosophical approaches or even reject them, are just as important. Future studies must definitely avoid examining the theological views expressed in these traditions from a theoretical perspective that allows for drawing all possible conclusions from them. Rather, it is important to look at what conclusions the followers of these traditions themselves drew and how these were reflected in practice (such as in prayers or other kinds of wor-

---

1 Wittgenstein, Ludwig, *The Big Typescript. TS 213*, ed. and trans. by C. Grant Luckhardt/Maximilian A. E. Aue, Oxford: Blackwell Publishing, 2005, 521–522.
2 The connecting line can be traced, for example, through William James, who was influenced by Native American thought; see Pratt, Scott, *Native Pragmatism. Rethinking the Roots of American Philosophy*, Bloomington: Indiana University Press, 2002. James' "Varieties of Religious Experience" was a book that Wittgenstein held in high esteem and strongly urged others to read; see Monk, Ray, *Ludwig Wittgenstein. The Duty of Genius*, London: Penguin Books, 1990, 478.

ship). This means that the respective views must not be considered in isolation but in their embedding in the larger network of related views and practices. Or, in short: They must be considered in how they are embedded in life. In his essay, Daniel Weiss impressively demonstrated, using the example of the rabbinic understanding of what it means that God has a name, why this is so important and how a theoretical approach gives rise to grave miscomprehensions.

These insights also apply to interreligious dialogue. Here, Muslim theology must engage in self-critical reflection on whether it allows itself to sufficiently enter into the thoughts and life world of the Other in order to get a deeper grasp of their theological positions. For example, Muslim theology often assumes that the doctrine of the Trinity necessarily leads to polytheism. However, instead of postulating such necessities, it would be more adequate to examine what conclusions Christians have drawn from this doctrine and how the doctrine is embedded in Christian practice. This is, because the meaning of the doctrine cannot be understood in isolation from this practice. Genia Schönbaumsfeld shows in her contribution that it is precisely polytheism that must be avoided from a Christian perspective. Similarly, just as the name of God in Jewish thought stands in tension with anthropomorphism, the doctrine of the Trinity may stand in tension with polytheism. But there is no logical necessity between them. This does not imply that the doctrine of the Trinity becomes acceptable from a Muslim perspective. Rather, it leads to a deeper understanding of the Other and reveals commonalities in places where they were not previously suspected. It is equally possible that differences emerge that were not previously in focus. Ultimately, this leads not only to a more nuanced understanding of the Other, but also of oneself.

Part Two

Daniel H. Weiss

Genia Schönbaumsfeld's insightful essay draws our attention to ways in which various people (especially some philosophers or some theologians) can be led astray by the outward similarity of different terms and can fail to attend to ways in which the underlying "depth grammar" of those terms do *not* all operate in the same ways. Aided by Wittgenstein's efforts to draw attention to such differences, we can be in a better position to note the ways that terms are actually used in concrete practices, which can in turn help us avoid drawing unwarranted conclusions in our understanding of terms such as "God."

Schönbaumsfeld notes that our use of various terms such as "beauty", "proposition," "one," or "God" have a surface similarity to our use of terms such as "cat," "table," or "chair." Due to this, there can be a tendency to treat the former as operating similarly to the latter, treating them all as "substantives," and simply positing that the former differ from the latter in being "invisible objects" rather than visible ones. This move can then lead to problematic inferences; in the case of "God," it can lead some to conclude that "if God is like a person but lacks a body," then God should be treated as a type of "mental substance." This leads Schönbaumsfeld to criticize certain thinkers' understanding of God as functionally treating God as a "gaseous vertebrate". By contrast, by breaking free of the assumption that all terms must correspond to substantives in the same basic way, one need not be led to such ways of working with or analyzing the term "God."

Schönbaumsfeld then engages with a range of interesting comments of Wittgenstein's concerning God and anthropomorphic-sounding language. In particular, she highlights Wittgenstein's remark: "So we may speak also of God's hearing our prayers. You might say then that in our picture of God there are eyes and ears. But it makes no sense if you then try to fill in the picture and think of God as having teeth and eyelashes and stomach and tendons and toenails." Schönbaumsfeld argues that asking whether God has a stomach or toenails is a category mistake, and that one can avoid such questions if one recognizes that one doesn't need to treat our use of the term "God" in the same way as we treat ordinary human beings, about whom we could indeed ask about their different types of bodily organs. In particular, she emphasizes that we should pay attention to the ways in which certain ways of talking about God relate to our actual religious practices; the fact that questions about God's stomach or toenails wouldn't have direct relevance to those practices can be an indication that such questions are an instance of language "going on holiday", raising theoretical questions that are detached from actual practice, and are therefore not amenable to being either affirmed or denied.

One interesting path of further exploration in relation to Schönbaumsfeld's analysis of substantives and anthropomorphism, however, is whether certain "anthropomorphic" elements may have a more concrete grounding in practices than other elements do. When Wittgenstein says that it doesn't make sense to talk about God's stomach or toenails, he does *not* say that it doesn't make sense to talk about God's eyes or ears, and in fact, he seems to affirm such elements as part of "our picture of God." This latter affirmation is tied to the fact that people do engage in the practices of praying to God and in the practices of exhorting people to act justly and rightly, since God can see what we do. Schönbaumsfeld suggests that saying that God sees our actions or hears our prayers does not mean that "God has strange sense-organs," but simply "serves to remind one that God is always aware of what one is doing." However, this may be eliminating the apparent "anthropomorphisms" more than Wittgenstein seemed to do. Wittgenstein appears to say not merely that God is aware of our actions or our prayers, but that our "picture of God" actually has "eyes" and "ears," even though we should not then extrapolate from this picture and draw conclusions about eyebrows, toenails, etc. As Wittgenstein says, "We know how this statement is used, and that is all right." Thus, while we should not treat the term "God" in the exact same way as we treat statements about human beings, we do not have to treat it in a qualitatively different way either: rather, if we "know how this statement is used," we can properly uphold both the differences and the similarities, even if this does not result in an account that can be analyzed with full theoretical consistency. Wittgenstein seems fine with a situation in which our picture of God could seem, from a certain perspective, to "have holes in it," and does not think that one needs to eliminate the holes in an attempt to make our treatment of the term "God" wholly identical with our treatment of words used in relation to human beings, or to make it wholly differentiated from our treatment of words used in relation to human beings. While this seems generally in keeping with Schönbaumsfeld's analysis, it may lead to a somewhat different direction in relation to certain aspects of anthropomorphism and grammar.

Farid Suleiman's engagement with the idea of the grammar of "God" makes use of the contrast between the "God of the philosophers" and the "God of Abraham." He suggests that this contrast, initially formulated by Pascal, can also be useful in applying Wittgenstein's criticisms of language-use to matters of religious language in particular. By understanding "God of the philosophers" and "God of Abraham" as labels for two broad approaches to religion, he enables us to trace the presence of these two attitudes within various streams of historical and contemporary religious thought. He argues that the "God of the philosophers" approach projects certain metaphysical assumptions and presuppositions onto its analysis of existing religious texts, terminology, and ways of speaking. This results in generating certain types of "theological problems" that were not part of the earlier framework of the texts and traditions. If the interpreters do not recognize that they are importing external presuppositions, they can be led to treat the dilemmas as native to the earlier texts themselves. Suleiman views Wittgenstein's grammatical analysis as useful for helping us to become aware of those unnoticed metaphysical projections and assumptions. Once we recognize that those particular metaphysical assumptions are contingent and not necessary, we can be in a better position to engage with existing religious texts and traditions about God without getting tangled up in the artificially generated theological problems.

Thus, looking at the examples of "God's existence" and "God's goodness," he shows the ways in which, particularly following the growth of *falsafa* and *kalām* discourses, various readers within the Islamic tradition have interpreted the Qur'ān in light of assumptions that the true goal of understanding God entails the production of a theoretical account in accord with logical and necessary principles of speculative thought. In relation to the question of "God's existence," for instance, this can lead interpreters to assert that the Qur'ān is concerned with those who affirm or who doubt God's existence. However, Suleiman shows that this may be a projection of the "God of the philosophers" onto the Qur'ān, and that the conceptual framework of the Qur'ān itself may not be concerned with such questions – not due to fideism or naiveté, but because such questions of God's existence arise specifically from particular metaphysical assumptions which are part of only some cultural-intellectual traditions, and are not a universal or necessary element of human reflection and reasoning. Importantly, he also shows that various interpreters in the Islamic tradition did *not* engage in that same level of projecting such assumptions on to the Qur'ān, giving the example of aṭ-Ṭabarī's commentary on Qur'ān 52:35–36. The fact that some interpreters engage in the importation of such metaphysical assumptions while others do not, highlights the fact that two broad attitudes to religion and religious language can be discerned within the broader Islamic tradition, and that one can trace the history of the relative prominence of each of them in different times and thinkers, as well as the tensions or struggles between the two orientations.

Moreover, by his focus on the details of the Islamic tradition in particular, Suleiman's analysis provides us with the tools to apply similar analysis to other historical traditions, such as traditions of rabbinic-Jewish theological reflection, or traditions of Christian theological reflection. In the case of all three traditions, it may be true that the scriptural texts of the Bible and the Qur'ān operate in a framework with metaphysical assumptions that differ from the "God of the philosophers," and that one can trace the degrees to which subsequent interpreters do or do not import certain metaphysical assumptions that shape their engagement with scriptural language and formulations. Indeed, while Wittgenstein's *Philosophical Invesigations* does not focus on religious language per se, it is notable that the opening pages of that book focus on what he calls an "Augustinian" approach to language – this itself can prompt us to investigate the ways in which Augustine's own approach to understanding of scriptural texts did or did not do so via an "Augustinian" understanding of language!

In addition to Islamic, Christian, and Jewish theological traditions, Suleiman's analysis and framework could also be fruitfully applied to the "Western philosophical tradition" itself, as an historical tradition in which various Islamic, Christian, and Jewish writers and thinkers participated. Could it be that there are some thinkers in this tradition who operate with the metaphysical assumptions of the "God of the philosophers" to a lesser degree than do others? After all, Pascal himself was a "philosopher," yet challenged the ways in which various thinkers had gone too far in the direction of the "God of the philosophers." This points to a potential ambiguity in Suleiman's analysis in relation to the term "philosophy." In some places, he seems to equate "philosophy" with "the God of the philosophers." For instance, he writes, "The Qur'ān is not a philosophical book, nor does it share the metaphysical presuppositions upon which the traditions of *falsafa* and *kalām* rest." I would agree with the second half of the sentence, but the first half is more questionable. It is certainly the case that the Qur'ān or the Bible is not a "philosophical" book *in a certain sense of "philosophical"* – however, a key point of Wittgenstein's is that the orientation linked to what Suleiman calls the "God of the philosophers" is not the only way of "doing philosophy." That is to say, Wittgenstein also views his own approach as "doing philosophy," even though it sharply diverges from many of the assumptions of the ways of doing philosophy that were dominant in his own time. Thus, it may be that the approaches that Suleiman calls the "God of Abraham" and the "God of the philosophers" can both be considered different ways of "doing philosophy," and that one should not inherently cede the term "philosophy" only to existing dominant ways of doing so, even if those dominant ways would also like to claim the term only for themselves. Elsewhere in his essay, Suleiman writes, "Philosophy and theology are, in [their] dominant forms, concerned with problems that would not have arisen in the first place if the differences of grammars would have been carefully considered." This formulation seems to take "philosophy" as potentially having forms other than the currently dominant ones. If so, it is possible that the Qur'ān or the Bible could also be seen as having a closer relation to "philosophical" thinking, when the latter is understood in a way more akin to Wittgenstein's own counter-hegemonic approach to the term. Suleiman's framework and analysis could thus be very helpful in future exploration of such possibilities.

Part Three

Genia Schönbaumsfeld

In his essay on the rabbinic grammar of God's name, Weiss makes a good case for claiming that while the thought that God has a name may be problematic in some respects, it does not automatically follow that such a conception needs to be perceived as "backwards" or as standing in tension with the idea of God as creator. Weiss draws on some well-known Wittgensteinian concepts, such as "family resemblance" and the famous dictum, "don't think, but look," in order to substantiate this conclusion. He argues that, when applied to the subject-matter at hand, these notions imply that Wittgenstein would reject as essentialistic and illusory the contention that there must be something inherently wrong with the idea of a God who has a name – as if it were a matter of logic that such a conception would reduce God to the level of created beings. To clarify, it is not that Weiss is claiming that such a thing could not be the case – that people could not draw such a conclusion – but rather that it would be premature to believe that it *must* be the case.

According to Weiss, it is primarily an empirical, not a logical or conceptual, question whether people draw the wrong conclusions from the use of a concept. At this level of generality, one might agree: It is not an a priori issue whether people in fact get led astray by a concept. Nevertheless, a concept's surface grammar may make this so exceedingly likely as to come close. As Wittgenstein tells us throughout *Philosophical Investigations* (most famously at PI §109) as well as elsewhere, the bewitchment of our intelligence by means of language is nigh on ubiquitous:

> We keep hearing the remark that philosophy really does not progress, that we are still occupied with the same philosophical problems as were the Greeks. Those who say this however don't understand why it is so. It is because our language has remained the same & keeps seducing us into asking the same questions. As long as there is still a verb "to be" that looks as though it functions in the same way as "to eat" and "to drink", as long as we still have the adjectives "identical," "true", "false," "possible", as long as we continue to talk of a river of time & an expanse of space, etc., etc., people will keep stumbling over the same [puzzling] difficulties & star[e] at something that no explanation seems capable of clearing up. (CV 22; translation emended)

In short, philosophy has no end, because bewitchment by language has no end. We must constantly fight against our *Trieb* (drive) to misunderstand (PI §109); our tendency to get entangled in our own rules (PI §125). Of course, the antidote to this is not to eradicate the problematic concepts, as this would neither be possible, nor desirable, but a heightened vigilance regarding the conclusions that someone would want to draw from their use. For example, we should ask ourselves whether the idea of God's having a name, or the word "God" itself being a proper name (as some philosophers of religion and theologians contend), would push us towards drawing the conclusion (as is very widespread in analytic theology) that God is a particular; an entity, that one can, in some sense, "pick out" and address (as one uses a name to pick out and address another human). If so, this would, together with the notion that God is also invisible, motivate endorsement of the "gaseous vertebrate" conception – the view that God is a bodiless superperson (cf. Swinburne), or "the king among existents" (Nielsen). That such moves would not be seen as innocent by Wittgenstein is revealed in this forceful remark to Drury: "If I thought of God as another being like myself, outside myself, only infinitely more powerful, then I would regard it as my duty to defy him".[3]

Of course, if, as a believer, one is already alert to the dangers of subscribing to the "gaseous vertebrate" conception, then the notion that God has a name will, perhaps, not tempt one down this path. But the perceived tension with the idea of a transcendent God may nevertheless worry one – it may make one puzzle over the question of how such a God can have a name like a Greek god (of which there were many). In other words, the notion could actively reinforce a problematic, anthropomorphic way of thinking about God, especially in those already prone to adopting such a view.

In this respect, I am also not sure that Heschel's distinction between a name and a notion is terribly helpful. Someone who has a "notion" of God – i.e., for example, has some understanding of the concept – need not thereby also believe in God. To have a concept and to believe the concept is instantiated are two entirely different things (otherwise the ontological argument would be valid). But this distinction is a purely logical one that tells us nothing about the nature of God or about whether it is appropriate for God to have a name.

What is more, use of the word "Father", or, indeed "*Adonai*", seems entirely sufficient to make an "interpersonal" relationship possible; the idea that God also has a proper name – especially one that can virtually never be used – appears not to add to the "I – thou" relation. If anything, in my view, it detracts from it. For the use of relational terms, such as "Father", put the emphasis on the relationship the believer has to God (e.g. on the believer's seeing herself as a "child" of God), rather than on the idea that the believer is praying to a particular individual who (perhaps) needs to be distinguished from other individuals. In this respect, it is not surprising that this notion first arose in a context where polytheistic religions dominated the scene.

Suleiman, in his ambitious contribution, takes on the "God of the Philosophers" – a conception of God as a metaphysical being, and of religious belief as essentially assent to propositions about such a being – a picture that he sees as exerting a nefarious influence on attempts to understand what is going on in Jewish, Christian and Islamic religious traditions (although his focus is on the latter). Suleiman sees "theology as grammar" as a therapeutic programme designed to free us from such misconceptions.

Overall, I'm very much in sympathy with Suleiman's project and there are many commonalities with my own conception. I think that Suleiman is right, for example, that the grammar of "God is good" is quite different from the grammar

---

3 Drury, Maurice O'Connor, "Some Notes on Conversations with Wittgenstein," in: Rush Rhees (ed.), *Recollections of Wittgenstein*, Oxford: Oxford University Press, 108.

of "my neighbour is good", as in the latter case one could base one's judgement on one's previous interaction with one's neighbour and his conduct towards one, whereas no empirical interaction with God is possible. I also agree that "God is good" can helpfully be compared to "all human beings are sinners", as the latter is similarly not based on an empirical generalisation, but serves as a grammatical remark and thus plays the role, as Suleiman puts it, of a "regulative picture". In other words, it is part of the grammar of "worship," for instance, that it is in principle impossible to worship enough. There could never be a state of affairs, even in respect of the most perfect worshipper, where God has been praised enough.

Although Suleiman does not spell this out, I presume that he would want to apply a similar line of thought to "God is good" – God is good, not because of any particular action God performs, but in principle. This might imply that it is itself sinful to criticize God on moral grounds (as, for example, Job attempted to do) or to try and exculpate God in the manner of theodicists (as I have argued elsewhere[4]). In this respect, it would be interesting to hear more about whether Suleiman's conception implies that it makes no sense to regard God as a member of our moral community, and, if so, what consequences this has. For example, would we have to conclude that God cannot be characterized as "good" or "bad" in the ordinary human sense *at all*? But if that is indeed the case, how, exactly, should we understand the grammar of "good" in this "divine" context, and why are we nevertheless wanting to employ the same word (as in ordinary human contexts)? Such an investigation would also constitute a potential further area of collaboration where a fruitful Wittgensteinian inter-religious dialogue could be had. For the notion that God is not subject to human standards seems to be another common thread that runs through Jewish, Christian and Islamic religious thought.

---

4 See Schönbaumsfeld, Genia, "On the Very Idea of a Theodicy," in: Mikel Burley (ed.), *Wittgenstein, Religion and Ethics: New Perspectives from Philosophy and Theology*, 93–112, London: Bloomsbury, 2018.

List of Contributors

Genia Schönbaumsfeld is Professor of Philosophy at the University of Southampton. Her research interests include epistemology, Wittgenstein, Kierkegaard and the philosophy of religion. Genia studied Philosophy and Modern Languages at St. Hilda's College, Oxford, completed her MPhil at Trinity College, Cambridge, and her PhD at the University of Vienna. She is the author of *A Confusion of the Spheres* (Oxford University Press, 2007), *The Illusion of Doubt* (Oxford University Press, 2016), and *Wittgenstein on Religious Belief* (Cambridge University Press, 2023). Genia is a member of Council of the Royal Institute of Philosophy, Associate Editor of *Philosophical Investigations* and Editorial Board member of Anthem Studies in Wittgenstein. In 2023, she was awarded a highly prestigious 2.5m EUR ERC Advanced Grant for her project, 'The Ethics of Doubt – Kierkegaard, Scepticism and Conspiracy Theory'.

Mira Sievers is a Professor of Islamic Theology at the University of Hamburg. Her research focuses on Islamic Ethics, Qur'anic Studies, Kalām theology, and inter-faith relations. She pursued her studies in Islamic Theology, Islamic Studies, and Linguistics at Goethe University Frankfurt, as well as at the School of Oriental and African Studies (SOAS), University of London. In 2018, she earned her doctorate from Goethe University Frankfurt, where she subsequently served as the academic coordinator of the Linked Open Tafsīr research group, focusing on the formation dynamics of the Qur'an. From 2020 to 2024, she held a Junior Professorship for Islamic Foundations of Belief, Philosophy, and Ethics at Humboldt University of Berlin. Her recent publications include: *Schöpfung zwischen Koran und Kalām. Ansätze einer Koranischen Theologie* ("Creation between the Qur'an and Kalām: Approaches to Qur'anic Theology"), Berlin: EB-Verlag, 2019 and the volume, co-edited with Rana Alsoufi and Serdar Kurnaz, *Wege zu einer Ethik: Neue Ansätze aus Theologie und Recht zwischen modernen Herausforderungen und islamischer Tradition* ("Paths to Ethics: New Approaches from Theology and Law between Modern Challenges and Islamic Tradition"), Baden-Baden: Nomos, 2023.

Farid Suleiman serves as Lecturer in Islamic Theology at the theological faculty of Greifswald University in Germany. He studied Education and Philosophy at Ludwig-Maximilians-University Munich, *al-Fiqh wa-uṣūluh* (Islamic Law and its Theory) at al-Madinah University in Malaysia, and Islamic Studies at Leiden University. In 2017, he earned his doctorate from Friedrich-Alexander-University Erlangen-Nuremberg. His doctoral dissertation constitutes a comprehensive exploration of Ibn Taymiyya's doctrine of the divine attributes, which has been published by De Gruyter (2019, in German) and Brill (2024, English translation).

Daniel H. Weiss is Polonsky-Coexist Senior Lecturer in Jewish Studies, Faculty of Divinity, University of Cambridge. He is author of *Paradox and the Prophets: Hermann Cohen and the Indirect Communication of Religion* (2012) and *Modern Jewish Philosophy and the Politics of Divine Violence* (2023), among other publications, and co-editor of multiple books, including *Scripture and Violence* (2020) and *Tsimtsum and Modernity* (2021). Actively involved in the Cambridge Interfaith Programme, he is a recent recipient of a Humboldt Research Fellowship for Experienced Researchers.

https://doi.org/10.1515/9783111501611-006

Index of Persons

https://doi.org/10.1515/9783111501611-007

Index of Subjects

https://doi.org/10.1515/9783111501611-008

www.ingramcontent.com/pod-product-compliance
Lightning Source LLC
Jackson TN
JSHW080857211224
75817JS00003B/104